This special edition of *Wellbeing at Work* has been published for a London Business Forum event in 2019.

LONDON BUSINESS FORUM

About London Business Forum

Founded in 2002, London Business Forum offers a programme of fun and insightful events presented by some of the world's most inspiring people.

You can find out more at www.londonbusinessforum.com

email: info@londonbusinessforum.com

Wellbeing at Work

How to design, implement and evaluate an effective strategy

Ian Hesketh and Cary Cooper

Publisher's note

Every possible effort has been made to ensure that the information contained in this book is accurate at the time of going to press, and the publishers and authors cannot accept responsibility for any errors or omissions, however caused. No responsibility for loss or damage occasioned to any person acting, or refraining from action, as a result of the material in this publication can be accepted by the editor, the publisher or the author.

First published in Great Britain and the United States in 2019 by Kogan Page Limited

2nd Floor, 45 Gee Street	c/o Martin P Hill Consulting	4737/23 Ansari Road
London	122 W 27th St, 10th Floor	Daryaganj
EC1V 3RS	New York, NY 10001	New Delhi 110002
United Kingdom	USA	India

www.koganpage.com

© Ian Hesketh and Cary Cooper, 2019

The right of Ian Hesketh and Cary Cooper to be identified as the authors of this work has been asserted by them in accordance with the Copyright, Designs and Patents Act 1988.

ISBNs

Hardback	978 0 7494 9775 0
Paperback	978 0 7494 8068 4
Ebook	978 0 7494 8069 1

British Library Cataloguing-in-Publication Data

A CIP record for this book is available from the British Library.

Library of Congress Cataloging-in-Publication Data

Names: Cooper, Cary L., author. | Hesketh, Ian, author.
Title: Wellbeing at work : how to design, implement and evaluate an effective
     strategy / Cary Cooper and Ian Hesketh.
Description: London ; New York : Kogan Page, 2019. | Includes bibliographical
     references.
Identifiers: LCCN 2018036797 (print) | LCCN 2018039524 (ebook) | ISBN
     9780749480691 (Ebook) | ISBN 9780749480684 (pbk.)
Subjects: LCSH: Job stress. | Quality of work life. | Personnel management.
Classification: LCC HF5548.85 (ebook) | LCC HF5548.85 .C6573 2019 (print) |
     DDC 658.3/12–dc23
LC record available at https://lccn.loc.gov/2018036797

Typeset by Integra Software Services, Pondicherry
Print production managed by Jellyfish
Printed and bound by CPI Group (UK) Ltd, Croydon, CR0 4YY

CONTENTS

Introduction

Stress at work is rising year on year, with long working hours seemingly becoming the norm. Absenteeism, presenteeism and leaveism are reportedly increasing across all industries. This is not only having a detrimental effect on employee health, happiness and productivity, but also impacting on the organization's bottom line. Human resources (HR) professionals are uniquely placed to manage this modern workplace crisis by implementing a wellbeing strategy in the workplace. As noted by Professor Dame Carol Black, 'The business case for investment in the health and wellbeing of employees is inadequately understood by employers' (2008).

This book is an essential, practical guide to designing and implementing an effective strategy, which will reduce employee anxiety, increase staff engagement and improve overall productivity. It is intended to be a reference book, as well as an initial end-to-end guide to setting up a wellbeing strategy and working through the process of embedding wellbeing in your organization.

The chapters, as detailed below, can also be utilized as individual points of reference for dealing with specific issues related to workplace wellbeing. These include common challenges, managing wellbeing through change and evaluating wellbeing initiatives, to name just a few.

Book structure

Chapter 1: Why wellbeing, why now?

This chapter sets the scene for the strategic importance of having in place an effective people approach. We draw on a myriad of contemporary thought to illustrate how getting this vital aspect of workplace strategy right can improve operational performance, and can lead to reduced sickness, increased discretionary effort, trust and employee loyalty. We examine and describe some of the new ways of working, posing a number of considerations for those charged with people management responsibilities, as well as those simply focused on looking after their fellow workers. We identify and discuss strategies to deal with key challenges such as an ageing workforce, remote working and the huge impact that technology has in the workplace. Most importantly we highlight how addressing the wellbeing issues related to these aspects of work can pay huge dividends, and why they should be included in an overall practical strategy. We have concluded this opening chapter with a look at the modern-day working environment, and the challenges faced by both employees and employers as they work to cope with a fast-changing world of work. We provide some illustrations to help identify how the criticality of wellbeing impacts on productivity, performance, engagement and discretionary effort.

Setting the scene for the following chapters that detail exactly what to do and include, this chapter highlights, to quote Simon Sinek (2009), the 'why?' The next chapter begins to take a look at how to get started on wellbeing, and what are the key areas to consider. These include that all-important aspect of having the right leaders; creating the right working environment, one that is conducive to good workplace wellbeing; and, finally, what makes up personal resilience. Unpacking these and following a systematic approach can be of real benefit for both employees and employers alike.

Chapter 2: Getting started

This chapter outlines the importance of getting a good team of HR professionals involved in strategy setting, and the importance of understanding your people. We explain the importance of creating the right environment for resilient and well-led staff to prosper, taking a detailed look at the leadership qualities required. First we take a look at the critical areas for wellbeing, those being to lead a meaningful and purposeful working life. We look at what constitutes that, and how creating the right environment in which that can exist is vital for employee wellbeing. Here you will find evidence and clear direction of what needs to be included in a wellbeing strategy, and why.

Drawing on everyday scenarios this chapter provides practical and graphic accounts from successful plans, allowing the reader to see success in action and to learn from the examples provided. To conclude this chapter, which we hope you will find both informative and insightful, we sum up the key aspects to any wellbeing strategy, the 'must haves'. We propose that creating the right environment in the workplace, one where employees can experience genuine, authentic meaning and purpose in their working lives, has to include the following dimensions. There must be leadership alignment to the business and the values of the organization. We suggest that investment in line-manager training that focuses on how to treat people with dignity and respect, fostering a growth mindset and allowing innovation and creativity will produce huge dividends. We provide illustrations to explain leadership through a transformational framework and suggest ways in which these sometimes complex descriptions can be simplified and brought to life in the workplace, inspiring and motivating employees, to quote Bass (1985), to work 'beyond expectations'. In other words, to employ discretionary effort, having established a strong identity with the working environment, where they are happy, have good relationships, feel trusted and valued and that the organization fits with their meaning and purpose in working life.

We also view some elements of leadership that are incongruent with wellbeing, giving line managers an insight into what not to do if seeking to enhance wellbeing. These too, we feel, are valuable contributions, allowing those charged with people responsibilities to impose order on how they go about leading.

Our final aspect of this chapter takes a quick look at the main aspects of resilience, and the fact that this pays a key role in all we do, both inside and outside of work. It is important to note that resilience is not like a tap, where one can switch on or download a measured dose; it is far more complex than that. Our next chapter explores resilience in far greater depth, indicating the importance we attach to this particular aspect of wellbeing.

Chapter 3: Promoting workplace wellbeing

Marketing the wellbeing plan effectively is often overlooked. This part of the book provides insight into how to avoid this, and gives valuable advice garnered from our considerable collective knowledge in the field. The criticality of effective workforce wellbeing plans is key to business success, and this continuous focus on professional development will help practitioners link wellbeing to leadership, ethics and integrity – allowing your business to remain competitive and have a strong social responsibility ethic underpinning practice.

The chapter begins by taking a detailed look at personal resilience. Following on from Chapter 2 we debate just what this may look like in practice, using the Resilience Prescription as a framework from which to plan activity. We then take a closer look at engagement, and how that is equally as important in the delivery of an effective wellbeing strategy.

We explore the promotion of workplace wellbeing – in other words, what's in it for the people? Although it is not always about what people will gain, or not lose, from a situation, we think it is critical that the benefits of promoting wellbeing are clearly defined. This vital component is worthy of detailed exploration, as it clearly links to how people in the workforce can make their life better, and connect to the meaning and purpose that is so important to leading a healthy and successful working life.

Chapter 4: Problems and pitfalls

Very often we hear about people issues effectively bringing companies to their knees, in both the public and private arenas. The purpose of this chapter is to draw your attention to some of the common problems and pitfalls we have seen when trying to implement a workforce wellbeing approach. Here the focus is on what success looks like, viewed through the lens of failure. An internet search will reveal the cost of sickness absenteeism, both in relation to direct and indirect costs. These are significant, and we hope that this book will provide you with the tools and techniques to make substantial gains in respect of these costs.

Employees being away from the workplace due to sickness is inevitable. However, research has shown time and time again that a lot of this is wholly preventable – though we concede not all.

An effective wellbeing strategy, implemented well and evaluated, can prove highly valuable. It also leads to a strong bond forming with the workforce, one in which they feel understood, valued and part of the organization; we have spoken of *identity* throughout this book.

We examine numerous accounts of where things have gone wrong, and the vulnerabilities of ignoring problems that – while they may seem to be surface issues – impact heavily on working life. We cast a spotlight on performance metrics, and the minefield that managing by these can be to navigate. We also take a look at staying focused and allowing room to adapt to emergent issues in your workplace. We detail the importance of having a positive mindset, and the use of sporting analogy by organizations to drive motivation in the workplace. We suggest that much of this is misplaced and can actually result in the opposite occurring over time.

The chapter includes a look at the intriguing topic of culture, and how this has to be fully appreciated in order to succeed in any business strategy, wellbeing included. A way to frame your wellbeing offering may be to focus on what your own organization does, and the mental and physical parameters of your own people. To help you work this out we have included some details of cultural tools that can help you make sense of what is going on, and how to ensure as far as possible that the strategy works.

The use of the Cultural Web is an excellent way to consider the requirements within an organization, and what may be the sensitive areas to be considered. This also helps you to think about best fit, what to put in place first, and who may be on board. The chapter concludes with a brief look at change management and stigma, and how these can impact on wellbeing. With many organizations orienting to a changing working climate, this is as important as other aspects we have spoken about in this chapter. Stigma needs no introductions really, but unfortunately is still prevalent in society. We provide some narrative around why this is so damaging and suggest ways in which the working environment can be improved upon drastically, reducing the stigma attached to mental health especially. A final word goes to compassion and kindness as channels to reduce stigma.

Chapter 5: Monitoring and evaluating

Revisiting a number of key constructs, this chapter aims to suggest how wellbeing initiatives can be monitored and evaluated, reviewing examples from practice and placing them in the context of valid and robust research to strengthen their appeal. We provide professional advice on what to look out for, how frequently to evaluate, and the importance of these processes in systematically reviewing your people strategy. Being open to challenge can be difficult, but we argue that workplace environments that permit periodic review will benefit enormously in terms of staff engagement and wellbeing.

We start by looking at the key advantages of strategy setting and what this can do for your organization. Taking a journey through the key elements, we discuss the strategic importance of goal setting in any business, and how that links in with your mission, vision and values. Constructing a strategy is important, and it must cohere. That is to say, that it enables the right hand of your business to effectively communicate and interact with the left – something that is not always apparent. We then move on to the all-important measurement of wellbeing – what that looks like and how it can inform any interventions or business changes you may consider making. Of course, these may originate from what you have garnered while doing these exercises.

The chapter then explores effectiveness and efficiency – after all, that is the aim of all business ventures – and will illustrate the key role that wellbeing plays on these areas of business.

We then look at performance and productivity, linking academic research that will hopefully convince you that the outcomes of a well-considered and executed wellbeing strategy will pay dividends, making your organization a better place to be. The focus then moves on to ethics, one of the cornerstones, and origins, of meaning and purpose in working life.

The chapter concludes with a discussion about evaluation. This is all-important – knowing that you are going along the right lines, creating your own evidence of success, and making meaningful changes for the benefit of your workforce based on what you have learnt. This growth mindset is where you should aspire to be. Having a learning culture, not seeking blame, but business improvement, should be the aim. We suggest this will impact on all the aforementioned and firmly place your organization in a great place – a place where people want to work, and where you accommodate meaning, purpose, happiness and prosperity.

Chapter 6: Tools and legislation

Returning to the purpose of this book, to help you design, implement and evaluate an effective wellbeing strategy for the workplace, this last chapter will hopefully equip you, or give you some ideas, on how to work through this process. We hope you may be able to use this part of the book as a reference for ideas, or as a manual to help colleagues understand better what it is you are trying to achieve, and also the benefits that this will bring to your people. The extensive use of good wellbeing practices benefits your business's performance and, of course, employee wellbeing. There is already extensive evidence from a variety of business sectors on the benefits that effective wellbeing brings for organizational performance, and emerging evidence from a variety of sectors on the benefits for employees. Good wellbeing practices enhance workers' skills, improve their motivation to perform well, and provide opportunities for workers to influence their work directly. These practices include having working environments that allow staff to have input into decisions about their work and their wider working environment (later in this chapter we discuss team exercises that can tease these out of employees). Good wellbeing practices also support workers with access to learning and development opportunities, feedback on their work through good performance management systems and encourage managers to support those they manage.

This last chapter, with a focus on monitoring and evaluation, will provide you with information on the key terms, the approach and how to view and assess what you are proposing (or are already) doing. We provide a series of quick tools to help you identify and resolve both long- and short-term people challenges, as well as thinking about more adventurous people-related initiatives drawn from industry innovators. This toolkit will allow use of this book as a reference guide to call upon when issues arise in the workplace that you are not quite sure how to address, or resolve. It will also help you to establish health-supporting work conditions and clarify processes such as attendance policies, exceptions and pay-related matters.

We begin by looking at some of the tools you can use. We then deliberate legislative requirements, what may be considered employers' responsibilities and those that could be considered the responsibility of the employee. Of course, this will be dependent on where in the globe you are operating, but nonetheless legislation is introduced usually to protect people, either from an organizational danger, or themselves. European working-time directives are a good example of this. To be clear, we see all wellbeing as a contract between individuals and their respective organizations. There has to be give and take here, otherwise this is unlikely to be successful. For example, businesses can hardly be expected to provide facilities to improve the health and wellbeing of their charges if people do not use them, or if they make lifestyle choices that put their general health at risk. This is true in reverse also, so it is very much along the lines of what we would describe as a psychological contract.

We also champion the notion that most wellbeing initiatives involve combinations of multiple approaches and stakeholders, and it is the joint working that really makes them work effectively; this is often what is compelling. With that in mind we have provided example exercises that can be done by employees, by groups or teams, and ones that can be carried out organization-wide. Using these you can look where your gaps may be, what causes concern for people, and what may leave your organization sub-optimal.

References

Bass, B (1985) *Leadership and Performance Beyond Expectations*, Free Press, New York

Black, C (2008) *Working for a Healthier Tomorrow*, HM Government

Sinek, S (2009) *Start with Why*, Penguin, London

Why wellbeing, why now? 01

Introduction

We have been writing about wellbeing for a number of years, and we consider that there is still a gap in the market for a HR practitioners' guide to conceiving, writing, rolling out and evaluating what amounts to an effective people strategy. The purpose of this book is to provide a simple-to-follow 'how-to' guide for those charged with people directorate responsibilities in both the public and private sectors, whether that be in HR, learning and development (L&D) or for people considering entering into this fascinating field as their chosen future careers. This book is also perfect for those who are just a little curious about what all of this stuff is about. Our focus is entirely on making it happen in the workplace, turning thoughts and evidence into practical workplace strategies. It is the Haynes manual for wellbeing and, as we have written about the 'people fleet' previously, this book will take you through the selection, ownership, management, servicing and repair of your most valuable of assets: your people. With practice in mind, we will cover all the points required to get a people strategy off the ground.

This opening chapter introduces the concept of wellbeing and will cover the importance of having an effective people strategy in place. This very much includes elements that will deliver wellbeing in the workplace. As a critical area of performance and productivity that is undergoing burgeoning interest, we draw upon the evidence base to illustrate how getting this right can improve these areas. Furthermore, how this can lead to reduced sickness, increased discretionary effort, trust and employee loyalty.

Wellbeing

It might be appropriate to begin with a brief look at what wellbeing is and perhaps, what we suggest, it is not, in the context of this book. Like any notion of leadership influence or management technique, wellbeing is subject to multiple interpretations. We ascribe subjective feelings to wellbeing – a state of mind and a state of being. These include feeling safe, comfortable, secure, happy, fortunate and, of course, healthy. Many commentators describe wellbeing in terms of psychological constructs of Eudaimonic and Hedonic. This book is not aimed at confusing the reader and we concede that descriptions can become complicated, but we think these two descriptors are more than worthy of further coverage. First, the Eudaimonic characteristics refer to the purposeful side of wellbeing – positive ways we live and view life, and our personal understanding and command of these phenomena, what we will refer to later on as 'knowing yourself'. These include issues such as having positive relationships, a purpose in life, self-acceptance and so on. Hedonic wellbeing can be described in terms of our pleasure or happiness, sometimes framed as subjective wellbeing, and again draws on positivity.

Happiness

The astute will recognize that, well, not everyone has a naturally 'happy' outgoing persona, and indeed this is a very good point. So, if you are not happy, can you experience wellbeing? To answer quickly, yes! Sonja Lyubomirsky, in her superb book *The How of Happiness* (2010), skillfully navigates the key components of what it is to be happy, including ways to recognize that you are, in fact, happy. The issue about walking around all day with a smile on your face is quickly dispatched and replaced by thoughts and feelings of 'non-grumpiness'. Sonja doesn't use this phrase, but we feel it fits quite well with what we are trying to communicate here, in that it is very much a state as much as a trait. If we unpack what it is to 'have' wellbeing, it soon becomes apparent that it is a tricky field of play, but it is almost impossible to try to isolate it from positivity. Another great author, Martin Seligman, has written expansively on this subject (2003, 2011), although a quick trawl through YouTube reveals that he himself confesses to being quite a grumpy individual. So it seems it is not about the outwardly reaching persona, but something much deeper rooted.

This is where, and why, it is critical to those charged with looking after people in a working environment to have a good understanding of wellbeing. To draw on Collinson's (2012) analogy of 'Prozac leadership' for a second, we could argue that leaders or managers who obsess about workplace wellbeing may find themselves equally as frowned upon should they take up an endless pursuit all day long of asking everyone if they are 'okay'. The skill is in being able to respond when the answer comes back as, 'No, not really.' Gulping line managers up and down the country may now find solace in this book as we unpack a selection of responses to this perhaps unanticipated riposte.

Positivity

Being told that wellbeing can have a huge impact on productivity and performance may itself inspire managers to view it in a more serious light, or simply view it at all. With austerity measures, cutbacks, efficiency drives, doing more with less and so on becoming organizational norms in seemingly most workplace settings, the skills of a positively charged line manager, free from stimulants, may be just what is needed to create a conducive working environment, one in which the workforce feels trusted, engaged and motivated to work hard. In return they gain an enormous amount of satisfaction from what they do, feel proud and talk positively about their work and their workplace, thus drawing meaning and purpose from their lives. These all seem to be essential criteria for any workplace, and so we suggest that getting wellbeing right can result in huge returns, and not only financial. These results, of course, need to be sustainable, and genuine. Authenticity in wellbeing will lead to a sustainable solution for the workplace; fads and flash-in-the-pans simply will not suffice here.

Psychological wellbeing

This is probably an apt juncture to explore a little of the 'ogicals' of wellbeing, having already briefly touched on psychological wellbeing and the sub-descriptors of Hedonic and Eudaimonic wellbeing, meaning and purpose, and such. Although we strongly suggest that psychological wellbeing, when it comes to work at least, is the area where it would be best to spend the time trying to understand, we will label and further describe the other main actors, as illustrated in Figure 1.1 below.

Physiological wellbeing

If people are asked to describe, 'What is wellbeing?' they are generally drawn to descriptors of the physiological kind. That is to say, being free from injury or physical ailments, keeping fit and being active. There is also the dreaded topic of size and weight here, BMI, cholesterol levels and blood pressure. Now, there are two points to

Figure 1.1 The four key tenets of wellbeing

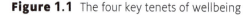

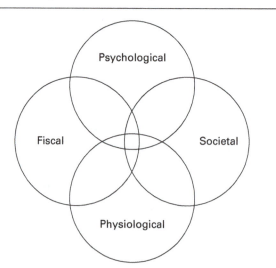

make when it comes to physiological wellbeing – and these may take you by surprise. The first is that the majority of people are not absent from work with physiological issues, well not primarily at least. The second is that wellbeing is much, much, more than the absence of ill health. As such, although popularized as the physiological, wellbeing does not take primary stage under this umbrella. Work-related wellbeing is most definitely impacted upon, in the main, by psychological wellbeing (PWB) issues – namely stress, anxiety and depression, all of which we will cover in depth in the course of this book.

Societal wellbeing

Our third area of wellbeing is that of societal, or sociological, wellbeing. There is currently much debate around measuring societal wellbeing, so we will take a little time to explore why this may be so. The main thrust of the measurement is that it gives the measurers, mainly called upon by their respective governments, an indication of the quality of life experienced by people in that particular area. It is a lens to look at how life is going for the masses. As a brief aside, the Organization for Economic Co-operation and Development (OECD) is very interested in countries measuring how they stack up on this scale, as an indication of what it is like to live in that country and, of course – and like with all measures – how they compare to the kids across the street (OECD, 2012). This fits closely with financial wellbeing, the final of our four related areas of wellbeing, in relation to the items that cover income, expenditure and so-called disposable wage. It is worth mentioning that the OECD scale covers housing, income, jobs, community, education, environment, civic engagement, health, life satisfaction, safety and work–life balance. We will touch on all of these aspects during the course of this book, and provide some idea about what good looks like, and also some practical steps to embed this in the workplace as part of a wellbeing strategy.

Financial wellbeing

This remains a major source of concern. Take the scenario of a young person leaving school and going to university to further their career options. During this time at university they amass what amounts to be a substantial financial debt that they can carry with them for many years to come. Added to that may be the relatively low levels of pay as they enter their working life and seek to become established, develop and progress up the career ladder. This progression may involve a transient lifestyle, effectively relocating to where the work is, renting accommodation and so on. These may be periods of hardship for younger employees, so we need to be mindful of that. Amongst the financial threats that exist for all workers are, of course, staff redundancies, job losses, splitting up with partners (especially where children are involved), moving house, inheriting debt or taking on loans that they struggle to pay off. What we suggest in Figure 1.1 is that this financial stress can very quickly have a huge impact on our other spheres of wellbeing.

Four conspirators

A closing observation on the Venn diagram in Figure 1.1 would be that it is very rare to see any one of these aspects impacting on individuals in isolation. What you would usually see – and for those charged with people responsibilities, what to look out for – is that they conspire, collude and round up on an individual. Someone may, for example, sprain an ankle whilst out for a jog (being healthy). This may result in them being laid up for a while, perhaps missing work. This then starts to impact on their psychological wellbeing, as meaning and purpose in life is temporarily suspended whilst they recoup. This could also, dependent on their employment contract, impact on their financial income. Finally, if you know people who are very much into their personal fitness and exercise regime and then find they cannot train, they can become quite anti-social – and there you have it, the four aspects have rounded and had a devastating effect on an individual's wellbeing. Now, of course we are not going to suggest that exercise is bad for you, but what you need to be mindful of is levels of resilience. This is something we will discuss in far more depth later in the book.

VUCA

The modern working environment was best described by George Casey, a US soldier, who made a valiant attempt at framing what most employers – although he was talking in terms of military operations – are facing today. He described a VUCA world (2014), where volatility, uncertainty, complexity and ambiguity are all part of the daily challenge. We capture these dimensions in Figure 1.2, and in looking at these areas a little more closely we can get a feel for the landscape facing our employees. Looking at these points in turn we can start to get a picture of what supportive help can assist in facilitating a good day at work for them.

Volatility is the nature and stability of the working task, things that are subject to change at short or no notice, for example – areas of work that can be either the very best, or alternatively the very worst, and are vulnerable to rapid change in both content and prospect. *Uncertainty* is a major worry for nearly all employees and

Figure 1.2 The VUCA world of work

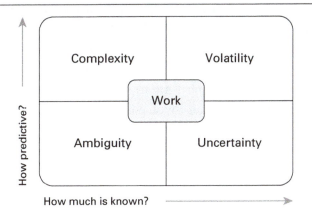

SOURCE adapted from Casey (2014)

employers alike, and has been the subject of much discourse. Long-term single points of employment seem almost extinct, even in some stalwart industries that traditionally offered 'jobs for life' such as those in the public sector, emergency services and so on. We will cover job uncertainty in greater depth further on in this book as we explore surveying the workforce, but needless to say it can be a major source of stress, both in the workplace and outside. In terms of *complexity*, we could frame this as the nature and volume of work entering our organizations. Can this be dealt with in what may be termed traditional ways? Or does it require a bespoke response, making it a 'complex task'? We look at issues such as the relationship the work has with other areas, the predictability of what may result, the number of variables present in the task, your own access to specialist help or assistance. These can all play their part in making 'complexity' a very stressful business indeed. Finally, *ambiguity*. This may best be described in the infamous two-by-two grid models popular with many academics and labelled as the 'unknown unknowns'. These are issues that have no set precedent, little is known of the circumstance or its solution, or even a range of possible solutions. Again, this can be a huge source of stress as workers process the dilemmas presented with ambiguity.

When it comes to looking at your workplace wellbeing strategy, models such as the one depicted in Figure 1.2 can help you frame sources of stress for your workforce and, perhaps more importantly, your own range of responses to those possible scenarios. This approach, scenario analysis, can help in two ways. First, it goes some way to prepare or negate emerging VUCA issues. Second, the exercise itself gives your workforce the confidence that you are, at least, considering some of the dilemmas that are coming their way. This has the effect of both preparing staff for the road ahead and, to some extent, allowing them to get involved with the subsequent response. It can be insightful to discuss these aspects with employees and seek response options from them, including them in decision making and strategy setting. As we look at surveying, later in this book, it will become apparent how vital a process this is, and the benefits it can bring to the workforce in terms of motivation, commitment and engagement levels.

NICE

So what is the likely future of work? The National Institute for Health and Care Excellence (NICE) in the UK issued a guidance paper (NICE, 2017) calling on employers to consider four issues in relation to the improvement of mental and physical wellbeing of workers. This approach, going directly to all employers, seems to indicate a deep understanding that the future of work may be very different indeed. If we take some time to examine what the guidelines advise it provides insight into where responsibility for health and wellbeing may be directed in the forthcoming years. It seems the broad-brush approach of 'employer responsibility' is no longer a generally accepted notion, and workers, quite rightly, now require a more nuanced approach. As in our previous look at VUCA, these guiding principles are also a most welcome addition for inclusion in a workplace wellbeing strategy. Hopefully by now the practical elements of this book are beginning to strike a chord.

Let us spend a few moments now to unpick the guidance. These were, first, to make health and wellbeing an organizational priority. The rationale behind this was to give leaders, and according to NICE these should be named leaders, responsibility. The aim is to display that organizations take health and wellbeing seriously and will support employees. In return, organizations ought to realize increased productivity, lower sickness levels and improved job satisfaction and retention. The guidance also suggests, in the second point, that line managers ought to have the responsibility for workplace health and wellbeing written into their role descriptions, thus formalizing this commitment. Third, what the NICE guidelines refer to as 'quality statements' refers to the identification and management of stress. This includes the skilling of managers in the identification of stress and a call for them to be trained in how to support staff experiencing stress. This is a point that this book can make a major contribution towards, as throughout we provide working examples of how stress may manifest in the workplace – what signs employees experiencing stress may exhibit, and how to address these issues for the benefit of both the workers and the employers. This, taken together with the fact that one of the most critical elements to any employment is one's relationship with their immediate line manager. We cannot emphasize enough how important this aspect is to anyone, in any arena, undertaking work of any kind. It is a fact that the line manager is the most influential aspect of a person's wellbeing in the workplace. It is often said that people join companies and leave line managers. Employers must feel trusted, valued and appreciated if they are to work effectively and efficiently over time. Once more, we point out the glaringly obvious that when this relationship is going well, productivity and performance is sure to follow hot on its heels.

Ageing workforce

The mean age of the workforce is rising and in this next few paragraphs we will explore why this might be so, but more importantly, the implications for workplace wellbeing.

Professor Martin Vernon, National Clinical Director for Older People and Person Centred Integrated Care for the National Health Service in England, has documented that our population is ageing. He has stated that, over the next 10 years, life expectancy at 65 will increase by almost 2 years. He has said that by 2025 it is estimated that the number of people aged 65 and over will increase by 20 per cent to over 12 million. Whilst for many this is great news, it is unfortunately factual that many people are living longer with multiple long-term conditions, which in part is contributing to increased demand on our health and care systems. Professor Vernon went on to say that in addition, while we can expect the overall prevalence of disability in older people to remain constant at around 20 per cent, the absolute number living with lost functional ability is expected to increase by one-quarter, to nearly 3 million people. Overall this means that by 2025 there will be an approximate 15 per cent increase in average years lived with disability. Most importantly, these population averages do not tell the full story. There is emerging evidence of significant and sustained differences in the trajectories of frailty and wellbeing between the richest and poorest thirds of the population across cohorts as they age (Vernon, 2017).

It is not beyond the scope of most to associate an ageing working population with a whole host of work-related challenges. These include mobility, technology, energy levels, sleeping patterns, medication requirements and so on – all of which have repercussions for those charged with looking after the workforce. What we also note is the inevitability of this coming to fruition, as the workforce dynamic shifts, albeit at a glacial pace. According to the Centre for Ageing Better, one in three workers will be aged over 50 by 2020, and by 2024 there will be 18 million people aged 60 and over. That is 3.1 million more than today (UK), which will equate to more than one in four workers being over 60 years old (Thomson, 2017). On top of this, the Workplace Report (Age in the Workplace, 2016) estimates that as many as 1 million people age 50–64 want to return to the UK workplace. However, it seems that the challenge of managing what appears will be an older workforce is still relatively unexplored. We see a point not too far into the future where it may be likely to have three generations all at work, top and tailed by a fourth, and even a fifth. A girl born today (2017) in the UK has a 50 per cent chance of living to be 100 years old. In a 2017 report based in the UK, the CIPD called for employers to keep older workers in the workplace for much longer, recommending an extra 1 million over 50s should be in work by 2022 to address what they considered to be a widening skills gap in the UK (CIPD, 2017). In terms of the wellbeing strategy for any organization, this will require a host of newly documented management skills, education and training. In terms of our previous look at the VUCA world, this dynamic most definitely falls into that category.

As part of planning how to integrate an older working populace into the workplace, those responsible need to be mindful of any needs, limitations and indeed advantages that this can bring. A massive amount of experience is instantly brought to mind. Being able to strategically deploy this experience can bring about huge business benefits, especially in viewing concepts such as learning by mistakes. It is not clear where the upper age limit will be set, if indeed it is set. However, there are most likely some issues around what is ethical or responsible management. As advances in medicine and health care progress rapidly, we propose that some of the issues facing the older working generation and employers are sited in their recruiting, retraining and in indeed retaining, which may need to be at least revised. To end this short insight it is interesting to note that the first person to live to be 150 years old has already been born. The benchmark of reaching 50 years of age traditionally signalled the later years of working life, and this may now not even signal the halfway point of working life. The Government Office for Science in the UK predicts that 12.5 million people will retire from work between 2012 and 2022, with only 7 million currently available to potentially fill those posts. This is based on birth-rate data and an additional 2 million jobs being created within that time (Cowley, 2016).

Technology

Love or loathe technology, avoidance is futile. With not a day going by without some new gadgetry being launched, a fresh set of operating instructions, increased digitization, and new ways of transferring things from one place to another, where it will end up the mind boggles. Today we have devices that can instantly translate languages, recognize songs, our voice commands and turn our heating at home on and off. One constraint is that at present these devices are oblivious to how we feel, if we are low or high. However, emotionally aware devices that can detect and interpret human emotions and adapt the lifestyle applications to match are being developed. The question is how will these be used positively in the workplace? For some this presents opportunities that are exciting and limitless, for others it presents the largest source of stress in the workplace!

If we look at workplace wellbeing and sources of stress, we would like to assume technology helps. If we take a look at your organization's printer policy, as an example. Where once you may have been afforded a desktop printer, conveniently connected to your desktop, or shared with a nearby colleague, is that still the case? Or do you share a printer on your particular floor, or worse? Do you enter a code, wander over to the printer to enter it, only to find it is out of toner, or requires paper? Or, is John from publications standing there printing out the *Encyclopaedia Britannica* for a few hours? This can be very stressful. So something that was designed to aid flow through a system is now blocking progress. Although we use this as a light-hearted example, there are many such cases where technology has hindered, not helped, in the workplace. In terms of wellbeing it is often a good reflection to think about the way work is designed. Is technology helping to its maximum potential, as we expect our employees to do?

When new technology is introduced in the workplace it can have two very different effects. It can make employees relieved that the once very tedious role requiring manual handling, whether that be physical or mentally processing work on an existing system, has now thankfully been replaced. Or it can make people feel vulnerable to redundancy or layoff. We will look at remote working in the next section, but this too often involves the introduction of new working solutions that negate the necessity for employees to be office based. With the redesign of a job comes a new psychological contract and this should be included in any wellbeing strategy moving forward. For example, if the workers that are being affected by a new working model have a genuine say in the new working solution it is likely they will take this ownership forward and be productive in the new arrangements, and often are more productive. We will discuss the management of change in greater depth later in this book, as this is one of the major sources of workplace stress and should be included in the wellbeing strategy. Communication is key here, and the workplace levels of engagement employed.

Remote working

The term describes both employees who are not physically in an office or workplace, as well as those who work flexibly and work both from home and office. This second offering is considered desirable, especially among millennials, with 35 per cent of employees in the United States stating they would change jobs to access flexible working arrangements. The Chartered Institute for Personnel and Development (CIPD) outlined a notion of smart working, which they describe as:

An approach to organizing work that aims to drive greater efficiency and effectiveness in achieving job outcomes through a combination of flexibility, autonomy and collaboration, in parallel with optimizing tools and working environments for employees. (CIPD, 2017)

One of the consequences of this is home working. For many this is the perfect way to work: maximum flexibility, convenience, autonomy, trust and empowerment. To some, in contrast, feelings of isolation, loneliness and abandonment are experienced. According to Gallup 43 per cent of the US workforce sometimes work at home, and they suggest managers need to get far better in addressing this. Humans are social creatures (well, most are), and although working remotely can provide enhanced levels of performance and productivity it can also create feelings of demoralization. So, it is not straightforward at all.

Although the challenges for managers in relation to leading a virtual workforce may be apparent, we will outline here some of the areas that may not be so obvious on an initial examination. One thing is for certain, there has not been any meaningful synthesis of the role of managing a flexible workforce, and it appears that managers need to become better skilled at this relatively new role that they may find themselves thrust into. Critically, the role of the line manager changes from person to task. That is, the manager often concentrates their efforts and attention to the outcomes and results, rather than the employees themselves. This is hard to do in a working environment such as an office, where personality plays its part significantly. This is why we often see people with huge personalities getting away with allsorts in the workplace, and the resultant productivity, or outcome, may be questionable. Other managerial challenges involve assessing workload, performance, and ensuring some socialization with the business; feeling like they have a working identity. Managers who have a remote, or virtual, workforce need to adopt different approaches in terms of communicating, assessing the varying needs of their directs, looking after technology and the requirements thereof; and also, how productivity or performance will be measured or assessed.

As we work through this conundrum it is easy to see why wellbeing plays such an important part, especially when it comes to finding meaning and purpose. What line managers can do, and which should form part of the wellbeing strategy for remote workers, is to foster a sense of belonging, even though remote. This means holding constant meaningful communication with the remote workforce, whether that be in person, via video, audio conferencing, text, instant messaging or other media that may well not exist at the time this book goes to press – the mind boggles!

The use of technology cannot be underestimated here; group Skype calls on a regular basis provide a good example. It may be that managers could also consider some 'online' social time, creating a virtual social community, so that this is not always associated with work, mirroring an office or factory environment for example. Managers can make sure that workers are kept up to date with company events, policies and direction, again negating any feelings of isolation that may creep up. It seems that lots of organizations, although working remotely, have hot-desking facilities to accommodate short-stay visits, meetings and get-togethers not related to work. This social element of wellbeing is an important factor for employees, increasing loyalty and feelings of belonging. To this extent managers may look at innovative ways of bringing the office to the home, re-creating, as far as possible, a virtual office environment, one in which birthdays and anniversaries are celebrated, there are coffee-break discussions, jokes, story exchanges and so on, which mirror the traditional office environment and empower employees to feel part of a bigger team and mitigate against feelings of social isolation or even loneliness.

We will touch a little later on work–life integration but, needless to say, remote working provides opportunities for flexibility. In that respect, the working day could be distributed; it could be early, late or night oriented. The appeal is in the flexibility and permitting that flexibility to truly exist. Research suggests that, perhaps counterintuitively, remote workers are far more productive and in fact end up working longer hours than their office-based counterparts. Managers should also be mindful of this, ensuring adequate rests and breaks are taken, that employees enjoy down time and feel empowered to, well, switch off their computers! A certain amount of face to face should also be aspired to if this is feasible.

Discretionary effort

Our final part of this opening chapter examines the phenomena of discretionary effort, or extra role effort, as it is known in the United States. Another way of looking at it may be the amount of work we do when no one is looking! When set against a backdrop of technology, ageing workforce, VUCA and engagement we can see how this can provide the 'tell-tale' of a successful wellbeing strategy. So, to gauge how successful you are with your wellbeing strategy, you can take a look at these extra-mile behaviours as an indicator of success. They may also help you highlight areas that are not going so well. The reason why discretionary effort is a good means of taking the temperature is that it is almost entirely free-will related to how an employee feels about the work they are doing, and the people they are working with. There are elements of charity and public-service motivation that impact, but we can push through those for the purposes of illustration. If a workplace has high levels of discretionary effort being exhibited across the entire workforce, it is usually a sign that employees are happy with their lot, and that they are drawing meaning and purpose from their working life. It is also unlikely that you will see high levels of discretionary effort alongside high levels of sickness absence.

To make the point, we suggest that you can have a work rate of anything between 0 and 100 per cent. We recommend that to push for 100 per cent on a continual basis will lead, almost inevitably, to employee burnout. This is not good for a number of reasons, for as well as the burnout of the employees themselves, the organization may garner a reputation that does not make it attractive to quality prospective employees. We suggest that managers ought to be seeking a commitment from people to work at about 80 per cent of their capacity. This makes it comfortable, achievable and unlikely to lead to burnout. If we take a look at operations management literature, this is phrased as the 'coping zone' (Johnston and Clark, 2008: 295).

As illustrated in Figure 1.3, if we ask our workforce what they can get away with, the answer would typically be about the 30 per cent mark. This is how much they have to put into the working day to

Figure 1.3 The hypothesis for discretionary effort

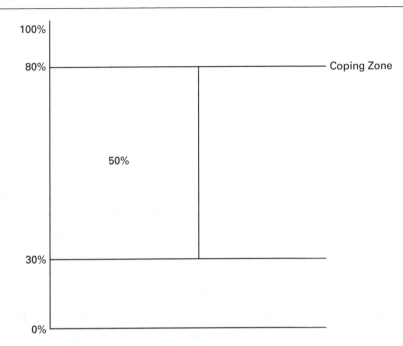

SOURCE adapted from Hesketh, Cooper and Ivy (2017)

avoid sanction, sacking or other punitive measures. This leaves us with a huge gulf of 50 per cent, as shown in Figure 1.3, that we suggest is given up for free, or, is discretionary effort. We hope you can see where we are going with this…

So, with up to 50 per cent of an employee's effort being discretionary, more or less, we hope you can instantly see that this book is going to be of immense value. We suggest that to tap into this extra role effort, an employee must experience wellbeing at work. We will now explain just how you can achieve this.

Strategy

So, the all-important question now is what is a strategy, and how do we do it for health and wellbeing? There are many great books that unpick strategy as a field of study. Books such as *Strategy* (de Wit, 1994),

Strategy Safari (Mintzberg, 2008) and, of course, *Exploring Corporate Strategy* (Johnson, Scholes and Whittington, 2008), now in its eleventh edition and one that has provided the staple for many business students around the world, offering more views on strategy than you can probably consume. In its basic form though, the consensus is that the strategy is, to a point, the long-term direction of an organization, although we concede that strategy is broken down into more sub-headings and contexts than perhaps makes it helpful. What we will stick with for our purposes is how to fit wellbeing into your business's long-term plan, the strategic fit, we might say. As we continue, you will read that there are a great many things to consider as you go about this. Some will merge seamlessly, others will take a little more shoe-horning. Before we get too far ahead of ourselves, let us consider the basic, high-level or corporate-level strategy, as Johnson and his colleagues suggest and as illustrated in Figure 1.4.

As you can see in Figure 1.4, the first thing really to consider is if this wellbeing strategy fits in to your current descriptions of what your strategic purpose is. If it is totally at odds, you may need to do some serious thinking about what this means for you, your employees and your business. You also may consider that this provides a convenient opportunity for you to revise or update your current strategic goals – a strategic refresh, you could say. For example, thinking about how wellbeing fits in to your current context, the current way things happen, your procedures and processes.

This leads nicely on to the second point, baselining your current position. Where you currently are can be quite an insightful exercise,

Figure 1.4 The high-level strategy

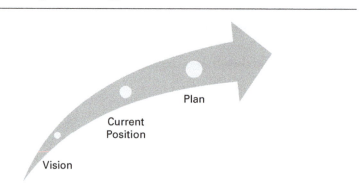

Vision

Current Position

Plan

and we have experienced a lot of businesses gaining knowledge by looking at their operations through a wellbeing lens. As we have already touched on, in terms of productivity and/or performance, a well workforce performs at a much higher level. This may provide you with an appropriate point in which to engage with your workforce, customers, suppliers and so on. Staff surveying, which we will discuss in greater depth later in this book, is a great way of taking the temperature. How do those involved with your organization feel, act and speak? You may also wish to document what is already in existence – what is mandated, legislated or practice norms? Do you already have initiatives that are beyond those which you have to have, and do you understand the impact these have? These baselining activities again provide a great deal of insight to inform your way ahead.

Finally, in the high-level strategy we look at the master plan to get all this rolling, including milestones, indicators of success, timescales and maybe more ambitious long-term aims. These could be aspirations to reduce levels of sickness, to have a happier workforce or increase productivity, and so on. Of course, each of these stages can take a considerable amount of time and resources, but we suggest that getting this right will prove of benefit in the long term.

Summary

To conclude, this chapter has set the scene for the strategic importance of having an effective people approach in place. We have drawn on a myriad of contemporary thought to illustrate how getting right this vital aspect of workplace strategy can improve operational performance, can lead to reduced sickness, increased discretionary effort, trust and employee loyalty. We have taken a brief look at some of the new ways of working, posing a number of considerations for those charged with people management responsibilities, as well as those simply focused on looking after their fellow workers. We have discussed strategies to deal with an ageing workforce, remote working and the huge impact that technology has in the workplace. Most importantly we highlighted how addressing the wellbeing issues related to these aspects of work can pay huge dividends, and why they should be included in an overall practical strategy. We have concluded with a look at the modern-day working environment, and the challenges faced by both employees and employers as they work to cope with a fast-changing world of work. We have illustrated how the criticality of wellbeing impacts on productivity, performance, engagement and discretionary effort. Setting the scene for the following chapters that detail exactly what to do and include, this chapter has highlighted, to quote Simon Sinek (2009), the 'why?' Chapter 2 will take a look at how to get started on wellbeing, and the key areas to consider. These include that all-important aspect of having the right leaders, creating the right working environment – one that is conducive to good workplace wellbeing and, finally, what makes up personal resilience. Unpacking these and following a systematic approach can be of real benefit for both employees and employers alike.

Key takeaways from this chapter

Wellbeing

We split wellbeing into two areas, Eudaimonic and Hedonic. Eudaimonic characteristics refer to the purposeful side of wellbeing – the positive ways in which we live and view life, and our personal understanding and command of these phenomena, 'knowing yourself'. Hedonic wellbeing would be described in terms of our pleasure or happiness, sometimes framed as subjective wellbeing, and again draws on positivity.

Psychological wellbeing

This is very much the topic that takes centre ground in this book, the wellbeing in our head, in its very basic form. This is how we think, process, behave and respond to others. It is our source of stress, both good (eustress) and bad (distress).

Physiological wellbeing

If most people are asked to describe 'what is wellbeing?' they are generally drawn to descriptors of the physiological kind. That is to say, being free from injury or physical ailments, keeping fit and being active. Physical fitness, size and weight, BMI, cholesterol levels and blood pressure are all physiological.

Societal wellbeing

Although there are lots of measures for this, what we are looking at here is how we are generally faring within society – our societal wealth, if you like. This can also be a descriptor of what our friend-ship circles look like, outside of the working environment. For example, whether we have outside hobbies and interests, people to care for, charitable work. Governments globally compare societal wellbeing, as we have detailed.

Financial wellbeing

In the modern age of technology, consumerism and rising prices, concerns around financial wellbeing can very quickly have a huge impact on our other spheres of wellbeing, so it is important to consider finances as a trigger to other areas of wellbeing.

VUCA

The acronym stands for volatility, uncertainty, complexity and ambiguity – an apt description of the modern era. All of these can trigger workplace stress, so this is an important concept to understand and become comfortable with.

NICE

The National Institute for Health and Care Excellence (NICE) in the UK is a body that recommends best practice in a whole range of health-related issues. Leaning on robust research NICE guidance is very much viewed as approved practice in the UK and can be depended on as a place to start if you are unsure about a path to take.

Ageing workforce

This is a considerable challenge in most countries. According to the Centre for Ageing Better, one in three workers will be aged over 50 by 2020, and by 2024 there will be 18 million people aged 60 and over – that is 3.1 million more than there are today in the UK. That will equate to more than one in four being over 60 (Thomson, 2017). On top of this, the Workplace Report (Age in the Workplace, 2016) estimates that as many as 1 million people age 50–64 want to return to the UK workplace.

Technology

When new technology is introduced in the workplace it can have two very different effects. It can make employees relieved that the once very tedious role requiring manual handling, whether that be physical or mentally processing work on an existing system, has now thankfully been replaced. Or it can make people feel vulnerable to redundancy or layoff. It is a major source of workplace stress and its influence can be polarizing. Love or loathe technology, it is coming at a huge scale and pace, so should not be underestimated in any wellbeing strategy.

Remote working

Another polarizing practice, remote working has seen an ebb and flow in some organizations. Research suggests that people are more productive and work longer when working remotely. Other research reports feelings of loneliness and isolation. Working away from the office via technological links is still relatively underexplored. In terms of wellbeing strategy, it needs careful consideration and certainly needs a differing management approach.

Discretionary effort

A further key concept, and one we have written about previously, is discretionary effort, or extra role effort, as it is known in the United States. Another way of describing it is the amount of work we do that goes beyond that for which we are rewarded, going the extra mile and so on. In terms of wellbeing, discretionary effort is viewed as indicative of experiencing meaning and purpose in your working life. It should be noted there are contrasting views on discretionary practice, mainly dependent on what your work actually involves.

Strategy

This is seen as the long-term direction or plan, and of course is the subject of this book. Planning an effective wellbeing strategy is critical to business success, so should not, under any circumstances, be overlooked or underestimated. We dedicate quite a lot in this book to strategic decision making and wellbeing strategy. Our next chapter will begin that journey of how to get started.

References

Age in the Workplace (2016) [accessed 4 August 2018] [Online] http://age. bitc.org.uk

Casey, G W (2014) Leading in a VUCA world, *Fortune*, **169** (5), p 75

CIPD (2017) [accessed 31 July 2018] One million more older people need to be in work by 2022 [Online] https://www.cipd.co.uk/news-views/ news-articles/million-more-older-workers-needed

Collinson, D (2012) Prozac leadership and the limits of positive thinking, *Leadership*, **8** (2), pp 87–107

Cowley, Science (2016) [accessed 31 July 2018] Future of Ageing: Seminar On Older Workers [Online] https://www.gov.uk/government/ publications/future-of-ageing-seminar-on-older-workers

Hesketh, I, Cooper, C and Ivy, J (2017) Well-being and engagement: The key to unlocking discretionary effort?, *Policing*, **11** (1), pp 62–73

Johnson, G, Scholes, K and Whittington, R (2008) *Exploring Corporate Strategy*, 8th edn, Pearson Education, London

Johnston, R and Clark, G (2008) *Service Operations Management*, 3rd edn, Pearson Education, London

Lyubomirsky, S (2010) *The How of Happiness: A practical approach to getting the life you want*, Piatkus, London

Mintzberg, H (2008) *Strategy Safari: The complete guide through the wilds of strategic management*, Financial Times Prentice Hall, Harlow

NICE (2017) [accessed 4 August 2018] Healthy Workplace: Improving Employee Mental and Physical Health and Wellbeing [Online] https://www.nice.org.uk/guidance/qs147

OECD (2012) [accessed 26 December 2012] Organization for Economic Cooperation and Development – Better Life Index [Online] www.oecdbetterlifeindex.org

Seligman, M (2003) *Authentic Happiness: Using the new positive psychology to realize your potential for deep fulfillment*, Nicholas Brealey, London

Seligman, M (2011) *Flourish: A new understanding of happiness and well-being – and how to achieve them*, Nicholas Brealey, London

Sinek, S (2009) *Start With Why*, Penguin, London

Thomson, P (2017) [accessed 31 July 2018] Fulfilling work is essential to supporting older workers, *Personnel Today* [Online] https://www.personneltoday.com/hr/fulfilling-work-essential-supporting-older-workers/

Vernon, M (2017) Ageing well: Reducing unwarranted variation in health outcomes, lecture at the Open University, 25 September

de Wit, B (1994) *Strategy: Process, content and context an international perspective*, West, Saint Paul, MN

Getting started   02

Introduction

This chapter outlines the importance of getting a good team of HR professionals involved in strategy setting, and the importance of understanding your people. Even if your business is relatively small, and you do not have dedicated HR, the importance of having people who understand how this can set the scene for all work is, we feel, a high priority. In this chapter we first look at the critical areas for wellbeing, those being to lead a meaningful and purposeful working life. We look at what constitutes that, and how creating the right environment in which that can exist is vital for employee wellbeing. Here you will find evidence and clear direction of what needs to be included, and why. Drawing on examples, this chapter provides practical and graphic accounts from successful plans, allowing the reader to see success in action, and to learn from the examples provided.

The basics

First, we would like to clarify that there is a fundamental difference between a strategy and a plan. You will need to understand what that is and take action in line with what your own business and your employees most need. If we begin by outlining the areas that impact most on an employee's wellbeing, we can then take a look at what measures can be put in place to address these areas. As with most aspects of life, where you take your lead from is of significant importance. Leadership in every organization is vital to both happiness and success. Next we will examine how leaders can create an environment in which work can be conducted in such a way that the worker extracts meaning and purpose from it. As we have previously alluded to, this can have a major impact on our life. The final area we will

Figure 2.1   Basic equation for wellbeing

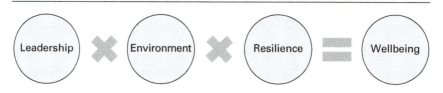

look at in this starting point is the influence of personal resilience. How enhancing one's own personal resilience can really make dealing with everyday life a much easier challenge. These elements are summarized in Figure 2.1. It should be noted that this is a multiplication equation, and as such if any of the elements are near to zero, the outcome will be low. Therefore, we strongly recommend that each element is considered to be of equally high importance and overall wellbeing will not prosper if any of these is low.

Looking after yourself in physical terms is fairly well established in terms of wellbeing, so before we dive in to the elements of the basic equation outlined in Figure 2.1, we might spend a little time looking at the areas that impact most on our mental health when it comes to a workplace setting. We will unpack surveying in later chapters, but needless to say the questions to be asked in these surveys need to have clear connections to an individual's thoughts, feelings and beliefs about their role in the workplace, their identity and their attitude towards work. As many survey responses are limited to attitudes and perceptions, these points are particularly important. We suggest there are six important elements that can be sources of psychological hazards for employees. As you will see, these correspond with the items in our [ASSET] survey. They are Balance Workload, Resources and Communications, Work Relationships, Control, Job Security and Change and Job Conditions. We will unpack these later in the book, but the areas clarify how employees view their own circumstances. Do they feel that they are getting sufficient meaning and purpose from their work? This is of vital importance, and ties to all the other aspects we detail that inevitably lead to happiness, positivity and the all-important sense of worth. As we progress through these essentials it is worth keeping in mind that you will have to keep a strong vision of where you want to get to, and maybe formulate some strategic goals that will sit alongside this, a list to remind you of where you are aiming for and, of course, why. It is not bad practice to have these on show to all employees and visitors to your workplace, be it physical or virtual (online). It is also important to map progress, what you are doing, who is responsible and how it relates to your vision. As we will probe later in this book, great leaders manage this really well and engage with people authentically. You may also want to link some budget code or financial mapping to your strategy so you get an idea of spend against return. A recent Australian study proposed there was a return of about 10:1 when this was done right (Milligan-Saville *et al*, 2017).

Leadership

Probably the most closely related association with wellbeing is that of leadership. Without doubt, the relationship that workers have with their immediate line manager is the one that can impact most on their wellbeing. This relationship can be the key to happiness, positivity, commitment, productivity and performance. Therefore, it is well worth the investment in your leaders, at all levels. In Figure 2.2 we suggest that at its very basic level leadership can consist of just three elements: knowing yourself, staff and stuff. Of course, having said this we can now look at what each of these areas consist of.

Figure 2.2 The three key areas of leadership

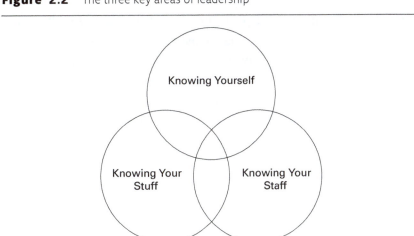

As featured in Figure 2.2 we suggest that leadership can be simply viewed as the ability to know enough about your stuff, staff and self to be capable of spotting when things are not quite right. This can be with yourself, or others you work with and for, as well as those in your charge. Further, knowing how, once spotted, you can intervene both quickly and effectively. This can be quite an art, and a science of course! We will now look at an example – that of bullying – to illustrate how these three aspects come together as leadership.

Bullying

If we take a look at what are definite taboos, it is easy to see how varying degrees of these traits can have a big impact on individuals. Workplace bullying is a good example of this, especially if it is part of a leadership arsenal. If you lead you have almost a duty both to ensure you do not behave in a bullying or intimidating manner, but also that others in your workplace do not either. There is also the very real issue about the subjectivity of bullying. Often dismissed or excused as workplace banter, one needs to be careful and sensitive to the effects on employees of whatever is going on. There is not a definitive list of what constitutes bullying, but it contains elements of unwanted behaviour (by the recipient) – verbally, physically or psychologically – that is viewed as humiliating, hurtful, intimidating or otherwise. It can be an outburst, or a pattern of behaviour, a single occurrence of which may seem innocuous.

So, taking the three facets in Figure 2.2 a leader could look closely at their own leadership style, maybe asking themselves if their words or behaviour could, under any circumstances, be construed as bullying or intimidating by others. If so, what can they do to change the way they behave in order to negate this? Also, if they witness others exhibiting these behaviours, what is the plan? Are they aware of the law, of company policy, of common decency to others even? Have they run through their plan to deal with it should it surface? This may include formal reporting mechanisms that should exist in mature organizations that are good places to work in. So, from just this one example we have unpacked what good leadership practice may look like and, more importantly, how this fits into the overall wellbeing strategy.

Transformational leadership

One of the popular frameworks of leadership is that of transforming leadership. Initially coined by James Downton in 1973 following his research into charismatic leadership, it was influenced largely by Bernard Bass, and his instrumental book *Leadership and Performance Beyond Expectations* (1985). Bass set out to unpick just what it was about leadership that inspired extraordinary achievement, and large contributions of discretionary effort. As set out in Figure 1.3 (Chapter 1), the benefits of tapping in to reserves of discretionary effort are clear, and something most leaders aspire to carry out. So, what are these traits that great leaders seem to have in buckets? What is more, can these be learnt, or are they something we are born with? Mobilizing followers while having credibility and commitment and creating job satisfaction, meaning and purpose for others is really the essence of transformational leadership. With so much change in business, and the so-called 4th Industrial Revolution in the making, it is clear to see that organizations can benefit from the approach.

If we now look at the four areas, although we concede there are many sub-divisions of these we can begin to understand what these leadership attributes may look like. What is more important is that we can start to define what it is you might be looking for in people you desire to lead your own particular work setting. Or, what development needs existing leaders may have. What is clear about transformational leadership is its congruence with wellbeing. We share the view that this may largely be down to the notion that it moves followers beyond self-interest, to see work as a greater good rather than simply a transaction for money, for example. In terms of wellbeing, you may begin to see how the concepts of meaning and purpose become more vivid. We look at the four main areas first, commonly known as the 4 'I's', these being:

1 Idealized Influence (II)

2 Inspirational Motivation (IM)

3 Intellectual Stimulation (IS)

4 Individual Consideration (IC)

These are usually compared with transactional leadership attributes of:

5 Contingent Reward (CR)

6 Management by Exception (MBE)

A last anomaly, which must not be entirely dismissed but fills in a leadership gap in the majority of text, is the style of:

7 Laissez-Faire (LF)

It may be helpful here to offer an explanation of what these words are describing before we suggest a simplified version for you to operationalize in Figure 2.3. Although when described, these facets of transforming leadership take on some meaning, we suggest that in these terms they are not, well, very usable. To overcome this, we provide a working solution that fits with our overall aim of improving wellbeing at work.

Idealized influence

This is a description that conjures up faith and respect in your leader. It suggests charisma, devotion, awe and emotional attachment. Now, we can see a little red flag here, and our good friend from Australia, Professor Ken Parry, suggests this may not be all good if one ends up falling in love with their leader, so a certain amount of caution is advised! However, broadly speaking we suggest that charismatic

Figure 2.3 Transforming leadership simplified

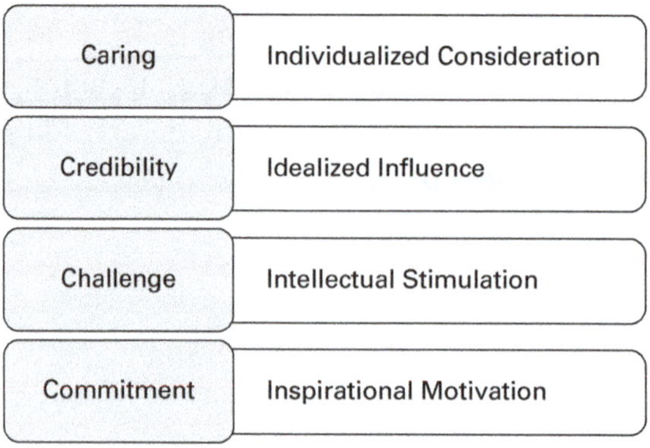

Caring	Individualized Consideration
Credibility	Idealized Influence
Challenge	Intellectual Stimulation
Commitment	Inspirational Motivation

leaders are attractive to followers, and make people feel good in their work, linking solidly to meaning and purpose.

This is an active and effective approach and, as in Figure 2.3, we suggest it could be simplified as credibility. In other words, what credibility does this leader have in the eyes of the follower? Sometimes this is quite difficult to describe. We may look to see if the leader has achieved great things, thought great thoughts, articulated great narratives, or is just a nice person whom people look to and like.

As the late Warren Bennis, an American author, scholar and organizational consultant, famously noted on leadership, 'Leadership is like beauty; it's hard to define, but you know it when you see it' (Bennis, 1989).

Inspirational motivation

To inspire and motivate are attributes that all leaders must possess. Communication skills and effective engagement is key to success here. Looking at our first point, leaders do not necessarily have to be charismatic to inspire others, they can have deep values, be highly ethical, champion a cause and such-like descriptions. People high on this are also highly committed, whether that be to an organization or a cause, or of course both. People can be inspired both intellectually and emotionally, through feelings, thoughts, needs and the ability to attach and align to their own meaning and purpose. When people see this in others we suggest it forms a bond, and in leadership this can be a powerful bond. It can result in high levels of loyalty, contribution and work satisfaction. There is a connection here to the individual and their identity, maybe feelings of being valued, supported and trusted spring to mind; that their work is important and valued as such. We suggest that this approach is both highly effective and active.

Intellectual stimulation

Work needs to be challenging. We often hear of burnout, but rustout is very real also. This occurs when employees become bored or tiresome, when the work does not challenge them either physically, mentally, or both. The role of the leader can really make the difference, providing the much-needed links to meaning and purpose. One may look at the role of education or teaching within this area, the role of a leader in guiding the way, through thoughts and deed, being a role model, having knowledge and skills they can pass on to those working for them. Referring back to the VUCA world modelled in Figure 1.2, the ability of a leader to navigate their workforce through these dilemmas requires problem-solving skills, as well as the ability to delegate, to trust, to support and talk positively about those in their charge.

Individualized consideration

This is our closest wellbeing area, and as such we show this as highly effective and active. This active element indicates that, like most things that impact on wellbeing, it requires time, energy, consideration and a deep sense of caring for others. This is borne out in the feelings of the recipients of this caring. Is it seen as authentic, genuine and long lasting? Another aspect of this, and one for leadership more generally, is whether it feels personal to each recipient. The ability of certain leaders to instil in others these feelings of personal focus can be very powerful, and often leads to huge payback in terms of work commitment, loyalty, discretionary effort, productivity and performance. As such it is a highly desirable attribute. Within this aspect we can introduce elements of continuous professional development, coaching, mentoring and career opportunities.

Transactional leadership

If we now take a brief moment to look at transactional attributes, and how they may manifest, we will see the impact these can potentially have on wellbeing, especially if sustained over long periods. The crux of the relationship between subordinate and lead is what the subordinate does for reward, or to avoid being punished. The reward may come in several forms, such as gaining financial reward, or not reducing, or benefitting from the transaction financially. In terms of psychological contract, it is probably the easiest relationship to consume – and be broken. Interestingly, the earliest forms of discretion, in terms of factory labour, were openly discouraged. This was largely due to discretion being associated with the freedom to make mistakes on the production line. The theory was that little freedom, or discretion, meant fewer mistakes and better quality; productivity was calculated as such and rigidly adhered to. Now if we take that and plonk the model into the VUCA world we described earlier you can instantly see the potential for problems. As such, we argue that discretion is good, discretionary effort is a clear sign of wellbeing, satisfaction, loyalty and happiness, and as such ought to be promoted and seen as good practice. One of the divisive outcomes of transactional leadership is that it can lead to deep-rooted competitive behaviours being played out in the workplace, gaming and other such outcomes. We suggest these are certainly not good for a spirit of wellbeing to coexist, and are certainly not sustainable.

Taking a look at these two aspects of transactional leadership brings to mind a couple of HR issues that may arise, or cause a rethink. Namely, that the reward and recognition mechanisms in place in some organizations, and how these almost conflict with these two areas. Remember, however attractive they may seem superficially, we are suggesting these approaches are not congruent with wellbeing!

Contingent reward

This is described as the means by which workers transact for reward, and how that reward may be given, or alternatively, not be reduced or withdrawn. Notions of piecework spring to mind, incentive schemes and so on. The employee works only on the understanding that they will be in receipt of reward, or will not be punished or sanctioned, as the name suggests work is contingent on the pay-off; an exchange. There is a minor exception here, in that the reward could be psychological, but we do not consider this a powerful-enough rationale to warrant a green light for this sort of approach!

Management by exception

This is a negativity-based approach. It can include negative criticism, negative outcomes, threats and coercion. It is akin to micromanagement, whereby in its active tense the leader is on the prowl for mistakes, errs and excuses for punishment or belittlement. In its passive use, the leader giving a bad appraisal out of the blue, without telling the employee when and where their work could have been improved or rectified, may practise management by exception. This is both passive and ineffective, and we suggest can have long-term psychological affects on employees, especially if they are exposed to these over long periods of time. Simplified, this can be likened to being treated like a child in the workplace.

Laissez-faire

The final leadership factor, or as it is sometimes known, the non-leadership factor, is laissez-faire. The astute will recognize it is a French phrase, meaning hands off, or let things be. It implies little or no leadership activity, no development, encouragement, no shouting, fault finding or anything. Nothing positive, but nothing negative either. Now, as we are considering wellbeing, this may well be construed as effective in some finite circumstances, for example where a team of highly specialized people are working on a highly technical piece of work, and the last thing they need is interference of any kind. A family business may also see this in a limited form, where there is no requirement for any interventions, development or otherwise. We suggest a modicum of effectiveness as there may be collegiate understanding that this is the case, therefore it is not ineffective.

Leadership summary

To conclude this section on leadership, hopefully we have illustrated a few considerations for those charged with recruitment and promotion into management positions, usually HR professionals. We have focused on transformational leadership, as more research has been conducted on this than all other leadership theories combined (Judge and Bono, 2000). What we hope we have shown above is the criticality of having the right people leading in an organization. One of the dangers is that operational competence is rewarded by a management appointment, and we suggest that leading people is very much a skill in itself and should be carefully considered. We have argued that line management is a serious step, and those taking up people responsibilities should be adequately trained, equipped and supported for the vital role they will play.

Taking into account the VUCA world we described earlier and the criticality of discretionary effort, it is easy to see why getting the leadership part of our basic equation right can lead to big dividends. As often quoted, the late great Albert Einstein is believed to have proposed, 'If you can't explain it simply, you don't understand it well enough'(Einstein, in Lau, 2011).

We have provided two illustrations above in Figures 2.2 and 2.3 that attempt to simplify what is potentially a very complex world. This is in the hope that it provides a memorable way of thinking about leadership in everyday business and informs the decision making that accompanies business as usual. Leadership is probably one of the hardest concepts to get right in the workplace, being almost a constant balancing act. What is commonly accepted is that positive leadership behaviours impact positively on wellbeing, and negative leadership behaviours impact negatively. We suggest that wellbeing provides a lens by which to make sense of the complexity of leadership, and thus renders it a useful tool for viewing and arranging work to the benefit of the workforce. We will explore this further in the next section when we look at what creating the right environment looks like.

Creating the right environment

Having read a little about these leadership characteristics, what now needs to be put in place is the creation of the right environment. This can be both the physical environment and the psychological environment; how people are made to feel. This is perhaps summarized impeccably by the late Maya Angelou, an author, poet and civil rights activist: 'I've learned that people will forget what you said, people will forget what you did, but people will never forget how you made them feel'(Angelou, in Rathus, 2012: 246).

We feel these words sum up perfectly what creating the right environment truly means. An environment in which workers can connect their own meaning and purpose in life to what they are doing in the workplace. An environment in which employees feel connected; they identify with the company or brand and feel energized in their commitment towards it. One of the areas that can provide a tell-tale sign for this is how employees speak about their organization outside of the workplace, with their friends or family. Are they positive or dismissive? Do they promote it, feel proud of it and feel like they belong? These are great ways to take the temperature in relation to creating that environment, and an avenue worth exploring if this features in your interests. In an article for the Chartered Management Institute in the UK, Sacha Romanovitch, Chief Executive at Grant Thornton, noted, 'How people perform is fundamentally part of the environment you create for them. It is about creating an environment that makes them flourish, rather than curl up and die' (Medland, 2017: 39).

We will explore a little bit more about meaning and purpose in the following sections, but for now let us look at an example of physical working conditions. As we alluded to earlier in this book, the working environment may well be a room in an employee's own home. In this case, we could assume most of the hygiene factors, as these things are known, would be met. However, an important aspect of wellbeing is to ensure this is how it is in reality, and that workers are not actually working in poorly lit, small and ill-equipped areas of their homes solely in the name of being a home worker. It is incumbent on managers to ensure working spaces are appropriate, and not suffered by workers in the interest of retaining employment or saving money. This can sometimes prove challenging, and of course conflict with the worker's own wishes. These environments may well not be congruent with wellbeing and require intervention on occasion. A good example is posited by the former Cabinet Secretary Head of the UK Civil Service Gus O'Donnell:

> Work is what you do, not a place you go to. The next generation of workforce will know that and be ready and able to work anywhere. Work has migrated beyond the conventional boundaries of time and space into a wider environment and those who manage the government estate need to be prepared. The office is rapidly becoming just one of a network of options, and for many people their work and personal lives are becoming more integrated. (Hardy *et al*, 2008)

To conclude, the working environment should be one in which employees feel positive, subjectively well (happy) and inspired to work efficiently and effectively; smart, if you wish. Although we will speak about resilience later in this chapter, employees should feel that their working environment is one that, to a large extent, increases or enhances their ability to cope with the work. Work is organized well, both in terms of process and ergonomics. A supportive, well-planned, well-thought-out and well-led working environment should feature highly and, of course, be subject to regular review and/or evaluation. Some great examples of this can be gleaned by looking at Amazon, Yahoo or Google and their original and subsequent approaches to home working, for example. This leads neatly on into our next area, that of meaning.

Meaning

This forms one of the fundamentals of wellbeing, the other being purpose, which we will cover next. The search for meaningful work is probably paramount in how most of us view our lives. To do a job of work that we neither value nor are particularly stimulated by is to resign us to a potentially miserable existence. Work can bring so much to our lives, it is important to be able to do work that is fulfilling for us personally, as well as seeing the broader good that our efforts can bring to society in general. This is sometimes balanced by our subjective outlook on what we see taking primacy, these being self-satisfaction or the good of others. Of course, these can coexist. If we look at the dictionary definition of wellbeing as the state of being comfortable, healthy or happy it immediately brings to mind why meaning is so important. Meaning, however, is not an easy concept to get right; it is highly subjective and can change as we progress through each of our lives, punctuated by events largely. We may have the search for meaning, the realization that we have found meaningful work, a so-called 'life-event' and then a renewed search for meaning taken into the context of the new working paradigm. This is difficult enough to both comprehend and manage on a personal basis, but what about how we introduce this into the working environment, as a manager? This is difficult on occasion, and one may have to generalize considerably in some circumstances. The work of positive psychologists like Seligman has provided some clarity to the proposition. He has deconstructed what it is to have meaning, splitting it into workable notions. His book *Authentic Happiness* (2003) argues that happiness takes on three guises – positive emotions, engagement and, of course, meaning. His later work, *Flourish* (2011), added positive relationships and accomplishment to the mix, and introduces the mnemonic PERMA to describe his notion. His description of meaning focuses on the service of something bigger than you. Of course, meaning is very closely linked to our next wellbeing fundamental, that of purpose. These are often grouped and used in the same sentence to underpin the criticality of workplace wellbeing.

Purpose

The bedfellow of meaning is purpose. This describes identity, values, beliefs, ethics and a host of other criteria that drives our individual passions, wants and needs. Much of this is dictated by our working life, the career we choose. That is if you are fortunate enough to make the choice, of course. Many are not, and for those finding their way, their purpose is a major quest. This is essential for our wellbeing. As Samuel Clemens, better known as Mark Twain (1835–1910), the American author, is reported to have said: 'The two most important days in your life are the day you are born and the day you find out why.'

Of course, our purpose may well change as we proceed through life, based on a number of criteria such as opportunities, life events, the needs of others, and so on. For managers, linking employees with their purpose in life can bring the 'eureka' moment. It can unlock huge amounts of productivity, performance and discretionary effort. It is also incredibly positive and supportive, making individuals feel an enormous sense of belonging and being valued. Of course, we can have more than one purpose, and direction in life can change due to a host of influences, some of which we have already discussed. Technology can have a significant impact; automation, intelligent help and computing power can change the whole operating paradigm for us. This can of course be positive, presenting new opportunities to explore in the workplace. It can also bring some avenues to a cul-de-sac, effectively firmly closing some life opportunities.

To sum up this point, meaning and purpose, almost always referred to as a collective in terms of wellbeing, are vital considerations when constructing any workplace wellbeing strategy. This is due to the sheer impact that both of these have on all of us. If we take how people consider work as an example, we can illustrate how important this is. There are broadly three classifications for viewing work, the first being a simple transaction for money. A straight trade-off for pay. You can see immediately that there is not going to be much connectivity, loyalty, devotion or otherwise here, in either direction. There are also good comparisons with the leadership attributes of transaction we spoke about earlier. The second of our trio is that work is viewed as a vocation, a career, a trade, a profession. Here the employee is committing to some level of identity with their trade, craft, occupation or whatever they choose to badge it as. There is a deeper sense of meaning and purpose, a connection to what they are undertaking. This is good on a number of fronts, especially for employers requiring dedication, loyalty and extra-role effort on occasion, and so on. For the employee, they gain an interest, a sense of pride in their vocation, a sense of commitment to keep up to date with their profession as new elements emerge. You can see why this is advantageous when we are viewing wellbeing. Our final view is that of work as a calling, suggesting some kind of deeper meaning, total commitment, loyalty and emergence in the chosen occupation. We often see this in ministerial work or charity-sector employ. Although one can see that wellbeing may be brought through fulfilment, you can also see the dangers of obsession, burnout and single-mindedness that can consume individuals, which we suggest is not particularly healthy in some circumstances. So, we can see that meaning and purpose are vital, but yet again individual and not easy to achieve on a broad strategic plan. Good leadership can deliver meaning and purpose in bucket loads, and we suggest this is where the investment is made when considering an organizational wellbeing strategy. This is also vital in terms of our next area, that of resilience. As mentioned above, our levels of coping are critical to sustained wellbeing in the workplace, and for the performance and productivity of our chosen employment.

Resilience

First and foremost, there are, of course, many interpretations of resilience. Coupled with the fact that, at some point in all our lives, we are all going to lean on our reserves of resilience, it is important to understand what we are describing. In this section we take a look at these holistically, and as we look into getting wellbeing off the ground in the next chapter we will look closer at personal resilience as well as some of the guidance we can give our people about managing this frailest of assets in our armoury.

The word 'resilience' has roots in the Latin verb *resilire* – to rebound. We can look at a number of interpretations here to try to get a feel of both the perspectives on offer, but also to emphasize that resilience has been researched for well over 40 years now, so there is a lot known about it. However, with this in mind it is also important to note that, in respect of how the brain works, Michael Taft, an expert in therapeutic neuroscience, noted at the 2017 Neuroscience Summit that: 'We have learnt more about the brain in the last 15 years than we have in the whole of human history' (Taft, 2017).

In terms of the literature on resilience itself, it may be useful to unpack a few of the interpretations. Resilience refers to:

- 'the ability to successfully adapt to stressors, maintaining psychological wellbeing in the face of adversity' (Haglund *et al*, 2007: 899);
- 'the capacity of a dynamic system to adapt successfully to disturbances that threaten system function, viability or development' (Masten, 2014: 6);
- 'the ability of an individual or organization to expeditiously design and implement positive adaptive behaviours matched to the immediate situation, while enduring minimal stress' (Mallack, 1998: 148);
- 'positive psychological capacity to rebound or bounce back from adversity, uncertainty, conflict, failure or even positive change, progress and increased responsibility' (Luthans, 2002: 702).

What is interesting here about what are recognized as the authorities on *resilience* is that they each refer to notions of ability and capacity – and this is important. Luthans's definition highlights the well-known and important '*bouncing back*' (or rebounding) aspect of resilience and is useful in drawing attention to the extensive need for resilience in both positive (opportunities or advancement) and negative (dealing with adversity) experiences in the workplace.

A further notion of resilience is around elasticity or malleability. In his seminal book *Aging Well*, George Vaillant, a Harvard psychologist, described resilient individuals as resembling 'a twig with a fresh, green living core. When twisted out of shape, such a twig bends, but it does not break; instead it springs back and continues growing' (Vaillant, 2003: 285).

As with the other aspects, resilience can be improved with training, and there is also evidence that higher levels of resilience can improve performance and enhance psychosocial functioning (Robertson *et al*, 2015), and as such it is worth taking note of. It should be noted that resilience is a broad subject, and many forms take place. It appears there is no conclusive body of knowledge to suggest an exact route to improvement, or indeed what works the best. To this extent, it remains very much at the fore, but still has an air of mystery regarding the optimum approach. We will focus more on resilience in the following chapter, but we felt it important to mention here as one of our three fundamental aspects to overall wellbeing and for inclusion as a header in any workplace wellbeing strategy.

Summary

To conclude this chapter, which we hope you have found both informative and insightful, we will sum up the key aspects to any wellbeing strategy, the 'must haves', if you wish. We propose that creating the right environment in the workplace, one where employees can experience genuine, authentic meaning and purpose in their working lives, has got to include the following dimensions. There must be leadership alignment to the business and the values of the organization. We suggest investment in line manger training that majors on how to treat people with dignity and respect; fostering a growth mindset and allowing innovation and creativity will produce huge dividends. We have illustrated leadership through a transformational framework and suggested ways in which these, sometimes complex, descriptions can be simplified and brought to life in the workplace, inspiring and motivating employees, to quote Bass, to work 'beyond expectations'. In other words, to employ discretionary effort, having established a strong identity with the working environment, where they are happy, have good relationships, feel trusted and valued and that the organization fits with their meaning and purpose in working life. We have also viewed some elements of leadership that are incongruent with wellbeing, giving line managers an insight into what not to do if you are seeking to enhance wellbeing. These too, we feel, are valuable contributions, allowing those charged with people responsibilities to impose order on how they go about leading. Our final aspect of this chapter has been to take a quick look at the main aspects of resilience, and the fact that this plays a key role in all we do, both inside and outside of work. It is important to note that resilience is not like a tap, where one can switch on or download a measured dose; it is far more complex than that. Our next chapter explores resilience in far greater depth, indicating the importance we attach to this particular aspect of wellbeing.

Key takeaways from this chapter

The basics

This sets out the basics of strategy, plans and leadership, which we look at in detail as we proceed through this book. This sets out the primary approach and some of the theory that will assist to move through and successfully create a strategy.

Bullying

If you lead you have a duty to both ensure you do not behave in a bullying or intimidating manner, but also that others in your workplace do not either. There is also the very real issue about the subjectivity of bullying, which is often dismissed or excused as work-place banter. There is not a definitive list of what constitutes bullying, but it contains elements of unwanted behaviour – verbally, physically or psychologically – that are viewed as humiliating, hurtful, intimidating or otherwise by anyone else.

Transformational leadership

The concept of transforming leadership, as it was first termed, was initially introduced by Downton. This was then developed into transformational leadership by Burns (1978). Bass expanded upon Burns's original ideas to develop what is today referred to as transformational leadership theory. His model (often referred to as the 4 I's) detailed the component parts, which we will now summarize.

Idealized influence

Credibility is the essence of this element. What credibility has this leader in the eyes of the follower? Sometimes this is quite difficult to describe. We may look if the leader has achieved great things, thought great thoughts, articulated great narratives, or is just a nice person whom people look to and like.

Inspirational motivation

People can be inspired both intellectually and emotionally, through feelings, thoughts, needs and the ability to attach and align to their own meaning and purpose. When people see this in others we suggest it forms a bond, and in leadership this can be a powerful bond. It can result in high levels of loyalty, contribution and work satisfaction. Steve Peters, of Chimp Paradox fame, argues that commitment is more sustainable than motivation, which can be short-lived (Peters, 2012).

Intellectual stimulation

Work needs to be challenging. We often hear of burnout, but rustout is very real also. This occurs when employees become bored or tiresome, when the work does not challenge them either physically or mentally, or both. The role of the leader can really make the difference, providing the much-needed links to meaning and purpose.

Individualized consideration

The key to this element is caring about the people who work for you. This is likely to be the closest in terms of wellbeing, and as such we show this as highly effective and active. This active element indicates that, like most things that impact on wellbeing, it requires time, energy, consideration and a deep sense of caring for others. This is borne out in the feelings of the recipients of this caring.

Transactional leadership

If we think of this as an exchange, you give me something and I will give you something back. One of the divisive outcomes of transactional leadership is that it can lead to deep-rooted competitive behaviours being played out in the workplace, gaming and other such outcomes. We suggest these are certainly not good for a spirit of wellbeing to coexist and are certainly not sustainable. However, there are (albeit limited) circumstances where this may be an appropriate approach.

Contingent reward

This concept revolves around an employee working only on the understanding that they will be in receipt of reward, or will not be punished or sanctioned – as the name suggests, work is contingent on the pay-off, an exchange. There is a minor exception here in that the reward could be psychological, but this is limited.

Management by exception

Akin to being treated like a child in the workplace, this is a negativity-based approach. It can include negative criticism, negative outcomes, threats and coercion. The leader seeks out mistakes, errs and excuses for punishment or belittlement. It is associated with micromanagement and may even be an antecedent of bullying.

Laissez-faire

A French phrase, meaning hands off, or let things be. It implies little or no leadership activity, no development, encouragement, no shouting, fault finding or anything. Nothing positive, but nothing negative either.

Creating the right environment

Ideally, a leader should seek to create an environment in which workers can connect their own meaning and purpose in life to what they are doing in the workplace. An environment exists where employees feel connected; they identify with the company or brand and feel energized in their commitment towards it.

Meaning

To do a job of work that we neither value nor are particularly stimulated by is to resign us to a potentially miserable existence. Work can bring so much to our lives, it is important to be able to do work that is fulfilling for us personally, as well as seeing the broader good that our efforts can bring to society in general.

Purpose

This describes identity, values, beliefs, ethics and a host of other criteria that drives our individual passions, wants and needs. Much of this is dictated by our working life, the career we choose.

Resilience

A broad area, but in terms of wellbeing we are describing personal resilience. The elasticity to return to a set-point, the ability to bounce back from adversity. The ability to store enough resilience to cope with stressful situations, as long as these are not completely overwhelming. So, we are talking about coping with day-to-day stressors.

References

Bass, B (1985) *Leadership and Performance Beyond Expectations*, Free Press, New York

Bennis, W G (1989) *On Becoming a Leader*, Century, London

Burns, J (1978) *Leadership*, Harper & Rowe, New York

Downton, J (1973) *Rebel Leadership: Commitment and charisma in a revolutionary process*, Free Press, New York

Haglund, M E M, Nestadt, P S, Cooper, N S, Southwick, S M and Charney, D S (2007) Psychobiological mechanisms of resilience: Relevance to prevention and treatment of stress-related psychopathology, *Dev Psychopathol*, **19** (3), pp 889–920

Hardy, B, Graham, R, Stansall, P, White, A, Harrison, A, Bell, A and Hutton, L (2008) *Working Beyond Walls: The government workplace as an agent of change*, DEGW/Office of Government Commerce, London [Online] https://assets.publishing.service.gov.uk/government/uploads/system/uploads/attachment_data/file/394153/Working-beyond-Walls.pdf

Judge, T A and Bono, J E (2000) Five-factor model of personality and transformational leadership, *Journal of Applied Psychology*, **85** (5), pp 751–65

Lau, J Y F (2011) *An Introduction to Critical Thinking and Creativity: Think More, Think Better*, Wiley, Hoboken, NJ

Luthans, F (2002) The need for and meaning of positive organizational behavior, *Journal of Organizational Behaviour*, **23** (6), pp 695–706

Mallack, L (1998) Measuring resilience in health care provider organizations, *Health Manpower Management*, **24** (4), pp 148–52

Masten, A S (2014) Global perspectives on resilience in children and youth, *Child Development*, **85** (1), pp 6–20

Medland, D (2017) [accessed 31 July 2017] Engage your core: The secret of Grant Thornton's new-found strength, *CMI* [Online] https://www.managers.org.uk/insights/news/2017/may/the-secret-to-grant-thorntons-newfound-strength

Milligan-Saville, J *et al* (2017) Workplace mental health training for managers and its effect on sick leave in employees: A cluster randomised controlled trial, *Lancet Psychiatry*, **4**, pp 850–58

Peters, S (2012) *The Chimp Paradox*, Vermilion, London

Robertson, I, Cooper, C, Sarkar, M and Curran, T (2015) Resilience training in the workplace from 2003 to 2014: a systematic review, *Journal of Occupational Psychology*, **88** (3), pp 533–62

Rathus, S A (2012) *Psychology: Concepts and connections*, 10th edn, Wadsworth, Belmont, CA

Seligman, M (2003) *Authentic Happiness: Using the new positive psychology to realize your potential for deep fulfillment*, Nicholas Brealey, London

Seligman, M (2011) *Flourish: A new understanding of happiness and well-being – and how to achieve them*, Nicholas Brealey, London

Taft, M W (2017) [accessed 4 August 2018] Five live-enhancing insights from neuroscience [Online] https://www.brainreframe.org/single-post/2016/02/04/Five-Life-Enhancing-Insights-from-Neuroscience

Vaillant, G (2003) *Aging Well: Surprising Guideposts to a happier life*, Little, Brown and Company, New York

Promoting workplace wellbeing

03

Introduction

In this chapter we explore the promotion of workplace wellbeing. In other words, what's in it for the people? Although it is not always about what people will gain, or not lose, from a situation, we think it is critical that the benefits of promoting wellbeing are clearly made out. Marketing a wellbeing plan effectively is often overlooked. This part of the book provides insight into how to avoid this, and gives valuable guidance and advice garnered from our considerable collective knowledge in the field. The criticality of effective workforce wellbeing plans is key to business success, and this continuous focus on professional development will help practitioners link wellbeing to leadership, ethics and integrity, allowing your business to remain competitive and have a strong social-responsibility ethic underpinning practice. The chapter begins by taking a detailed look at strategy and personal resilience. Following on from Chapter 2 we debate just what this might look like in practice, using the Resilience Prescription as a framework from which to plan activity. This vital component is worthy of detailed exploration, as it clearly links to how people in the workforce can make their life better and connect to the meaning and purpose that is so important to leading a healthy and successful working life.

Strategy setting

With plenty of books being dedicated to strategy we are not going to theorize to any great extent here but will provide examples from key thinkers on this subject. That said, it is important, if not critical, to ensure your wellbeing strategy sits firmly within an organization's general working premise. We suggest that fact-finding exercises, if it is not obvious, are carried out in a collaborative manner. Most research suggests this is optimum in terms of outcome. If there is an executive layer, primarily you need agreement as to what the general purpose of the organization is, and how wellbeing fits in with that purpose. Furthermore, how wellbeing adds to that purpose in a meaningful and contributing way. This must then be disseminated effectively. This is critical, as noted: 'everyday interactions of lower-level managers and ordinary staff can easily undermine an intended strategy' (Johnson, Scholes and Whittington, 2008: 574). Furthermore, 'middle managers in particular are likely to be key since they are often tasked with making senior management plans' (Balogun, 2007: 81).

Wellbeing must be viewed in a positive light; it is not something that brings an organization to its knees, quite the opposite. We have heard moans and gripes about health and safety, human resources, occupational health and so on being the bug-bear for senior leaders. Wellbeing should be attached to nothing of the sort. It is therefore important, if you are a largish organization, that it sits under the correct management area of responsibility, preferably an executive function – we would argue that wellbeing is that important.

In terms of review, even if the strategy is clear, and the conduit to wellbeing firmly in place, regular reviews should be scheduled in. As well as annual strategy reviews, it is good practice to look at wellbeing periodically in terms of best fit. It is rare these days for organizations to carry on day-to-day business unchanged. What we are suggesting is that if there are big changes, in size, policy, procedure, management changes and so on, a recap and communication of the wellbeing strategy fit should be highlighted as best practice: 'Deciding strategy is only one step; strategic decisions need to be communicated' (Johnson, Scholes and Whittington, 2008: 574).

As we have discussed already in this book, this has a positive impact on the workforce. Employees feel valued and cared for, so make the review overt, garner opinion, and let employees engage with the process: 'Companies must remake themselves into places of engagement, where people are committed to one another and their enterprise' (Mintzberg, 2009: 140). Also, employees are more likely to engage with other areas of the business if they are bought in, have interest, and feel part of it.

It is also helpful to have the strategy laid out clearly, accessible to the workforce and wider stakeholders (suppliers, contractors, temps, agency staff and so on). Porter comments that 'companies do not function in isolation from the society around them' (Porter and Kramer, 2002). In this way your people will know you are committed to their wellbeing, and will act and perform accordingly, 'for every new strategy, there should be a communications strategy to match' (Johnson, Scholes and Whittington, 2008: 574). Productivity and performance are some of the key outcomes for an effective wellbeing approach. Others will include organizational effectiveness, individual and organizational resilience, lower absence rates, higher morale and a motivated workforce. There is research to support all of these notions. At the end of the day, these help in terms of your business's sustainability. Most will agree this is a key priority in this uncertain period for businesses large and small. You may want to lay out a set of strategic principles, which can be a bullet-pointed paragraph or two outlining the landscape and the main aims of the strategy. These are usually followed with strategic objectives, which provide further direction about what you intend to do.

A further consideration, which we have briefly touched upon already, is how the strategy dovetails with other areas. How will it fit in with HR policies, legislative requirements, health and safety, your training programmes, and so on? These are important considerations, and we suggest that you do not simply consume wellbeing into other areas of business. We consider it has earned the right to stand alone. Although, it will impact on almost all other aspects in one way or another. If you consider the organizational timeline, from planning resources, winning contracts, financial parameters, recruiting the right people, progression arrangements, customer interfaces, production or service provision – you can see clearly that the notion of a well-functioning body of people to carry all this out has got to be a good idea.

Having, albeit briefly, outlined the strategic importance, and the siting of wellbeing, let us now turn our attention to what actually should be contained within the strategy itself.

Goals

It is most likely no surprise that any organization needs a set of goals, and in terms of wellbeing this should be no different. What is probably not as apparent is how these fit in with the overall strategic direction; where you want to get to, so to speak. We will discuss mission and vision shortly, but first the actionable goals. Goals must be, at some point at least; achievable. Setting outlandish or entirely aspirational goals is not particularly useful when set in the context of wellbeing. For example, goals such as eradicating all ill-health and such are unlikely ever to be realized, and employees soon become alert to this, and thus they are not valued, or aspired to. There is also the point of mixing up goals with the mission and values, and though often confusing they are, or should be, different things. So, the goals when laying out your wellbeing plans should be set around making life at work as good as it can be, or not doing things that would compromise an employee's health and wellbeing. We acknowledge that in some countries health and safety legislates for this. Also, be careful not to have too many goals in relation to wellbeing. You want to avoid this being a list, if at all possible, under the goals, which should be a simple statement of objectives outlining specifically how you intend to achieve this. The goals and objectives, as well as being achievable, should also be measurable. That is, how do you know when you have achieved them? What does success look like? With the end in mind, this should steer you in decision making about your goal setting. It is also important to keep in mind why you are actually doing whatever it is. Will these 'things' help the organization in some way? As well as the company being profitable, does it maintain responsibility for what it does (often referred to as corporate social responsibility)? The bottom line is that you should take care in defining your goals, and ensure they are both actionable and achievable. Monitoring the goals is relatively straightforward. The objectives set to deliver the goals should be drafted with enough detail to allow for the checking of progress against them. In the same manner, the evaluation of goals should be relatively simple. Ask questions such as to what extent have they been achieved, or are on track. Having such structures in place is not only good business management, but it also allows for detailed progress reporting when required. This makes life easy (less stressful) for all, and ought to be adopted as best practice.

Personal resilience

If we try to think of the brain as a great big chemical production facility located at the top of our body, constantly churning out different potions to facilitate a number of physical and cognitive functions, we can begin to see that it is incredibly complex, at times unstable, and dependent on so many variables that the mind boggles. One of the keys to understanding personal resilience may be found in the subject of stress. If we view personal resilience as a plethora of armaments to combat stress we think it may be just about sufficient to enable an understanding of the basics of personal resilience. However, it is complicated, and very complicated at that! To begin with, no two people process information exactly the same. Studies into identical twins have unveiled subtleties that even the closest gene match can bring, even though suggestions of telepathy, 'special connections' and feeling each other's pain have been posited. It seems the only real likelihood is an increased chance they are likely to conceive twins themselves. According to Professor Eric Kandel from Columbia University in the United States, although identical twins have identical genes, their different life and social experiences result in them having different brains (Kandel, 2017).

If we look at resilience as two aspects, the first is the ability to cope with the everyday stressors of life, the drip-drip-drip if you like. Obviously things impact on this in various ways, minor setbacks and so on. The second aspect is the ability to deal with a major traumatic event – when something goes horribly wrong and our emotional balance is tested to its limits. Theoretically at least, if our resilience is high then we can weather these life events and recover to working capacity. As the American Psychological Association defines it, resilience is: 'the process of adapting well in the face of adversity, trauma, tragedy, threats and even significant sources of stress' (Southwick and Charney, 2012: 7). However, as noted by Robertson *et al* (2015), the research on improving resilience is tentative.

Stress

It may be worth spending a few moments on stress here. Stress, the silent killer, is both a threat and an opportunity to push us to new levels. To simplify, when we experience stress, a *'chemical factory'* in our brain releases a host of various drugs into our body (up to 50 recognized) in response to a perceived stressor. Interestingly, if the perceived stressor turns out to be reality, the chemicals produced can be utilized positively. One of the problems arises if these are not real stressors, and we end up with a chemical imbalance, leading to anxiety and/or potentially chronic depression.

To illustrate it might be worth looking at some of the work of the *chemical factory* in greater detail. Probably the most notorious of stress hormones is cortisol, which helps us produce energy in times of need. Epinephrine, or adrenaline, is produced in response to the 'fight or flight' response, speeding up the heart rate and opening up our airways. Norepinephrine and noradrenaline fuel the parasympathetic nervous system, which counteracts (and therefore regulates) the sympathetic nervous system's fight, flight or freeze responses. It is the 'rest and digest' system, as opposed to flight and flight.

Serotonin positively regulates mood, sleep, appetite and other functions. Dopamine provides pleasure, reward and can load addictive behaviours. Neuropeptides can cause decreased anxiety that helps the body return to a normal state. Oxytocin relates to social bonding, love, attraction, trust and support. Endorphins are the brain's painkiller, known as neurotransmitters.

Counter-intuitively it seems that some stress is good for us, although it is often associated with being ill, feeling awful or not being able to cope with life. If it is moderate, short-lived and increases energy it can bring about challenge and stimulation. For example, we may by choice go on a fairground ride, a rollercoaster that propels us into the air, upside down, loop the loop and so on. Although this creates exactly the same chemical reaction, it is exhilarating, fun and maybe even scary. Most importantly however, the key is that it is short-lived. Continuing on with that analogy, if we were to ride the rollercoaster for hours it may not feel scary after a couple of circuits, in other words we will have become used to the phenomena that originally terrified us.

If we have an examination or a test, the anticipatory reaction of the body might produce chemicals that stimulate us, keep us in a heightened state, able to concentrate and recall facts important for our success, so called *eustress* (Selye, 1975), which is good stress that motivates us. As already mentioned, we all have different reactions to circumstances that are presented to us. Unlike animals, humans can activate a stress response through thoughts. These thoughts may not be justified (anticipatory) by any supporting evidence that we will come to harm, for example, a rise in mortgage interest rates. What is probably most surprising is that what happens after this release is highly dependent on factors such as social support, personality and personal resilience. The neural circuitry that effects our behaviour as a consequence of stress (Figure 3.1) is a fascinating area of study, and we will merely scratch the surface here. What we hope, however, is that you can see the benefits for employees if they have a better understanding of at least how some of these interact, and the resultant

Figure 3.1   Brain chemicals and stressors

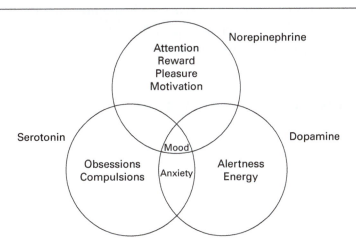

catastrophe if not managed well. Stress affects the immune system, our hormones, circulatory system, energy levels, growth, reproduction and life expectancy – just about everything. In the workplace it can impact significantly on productivity, performance and happiness (subjective wellbeing). To cope physiologically and psychologically with stress, good levels of personal resilience are required, and this is what we will explore further now.

Trauma

It may be prudent here to take a quick peep at the world of trauma, which can lead from a stressful situation and can be referred to as traumatic exposure. This situation can be the result of a one-off, or can be a series of things that the person subject to it deems to be traumatic. Note that it does not need to be traumatic to all people, just in the eye of the beholder; and can consist of what some might see as everyday events. Also, there does not need to be traumatic things present, it can be perceived (so-called filling in the blanks). Primary trauma can occur when the subject has direct exposure themselves. Secondary trauma is when the subject relives whatever has happened, or been reported, through the eyes of others, causing themselves to experience the trauma as if it were happening on a primary level. One of the more well-known uses of the term is post-traumatic stress disorder (PTSD), but it does not always follow that exposure to trauma leads to PTSD. You should note that the diagnosis of PTSD requires a specialist and, although the term is often used, the prevalence rates of PTSD are very low.

The Resilience Prescription

This is really about managing stress levels, what impacts on this, and what can be achieved to combat stress if it starts to become heightened. What we explain here will help you to understand how you can keep yourself and your colleagues psychologically fit, what we might call a 'functioning population'. When it comes to physical fitness, we would suggest that, relatively speaking, this is a fairly simple task. After all, physical fitness is easy to see, test, understand and usually to rectify. If you break your leg, for example, you go to the hospital, get an X-ray to confirm, have it pinned or put in a cast for a set period, rehab and back to normal, all being well. Psychological or mental illness is not that straightforward and comes in many forms and levels of severity.

The seminal work of Southwick and Charney (2012) looked at the science of mastering life's challenges, and set out to suggest the key aspects (the prescription) that impact on our own resilience. These are:

- a positive attitude;
- cognitive flexibility;
- moral compass;
- role models;
- facing fears;
- coping skills;
- supportive networks;
- physical wellbeing;
- regular training;
- signature strengths.

Taking these into the arena of what areas of wellbeing to promote, we will provide a little more detail on what you might wish to consider. These may form the core of what you are actually asking your workers to do, or to consider or strive to do.

Wellbeing and engagement

We now get to the crux of wellbeing, which is operationalizing it in the workplace. A lot of our commentary so far relating to personal resilience, stress and trauma is probably not too surprising or unexpected. Trying to launch wellbeing in the workplace, and making it meaningful for people and getting them to engage in the delivery and success is, however, the more difficult part. This is why an effective engagement strategy is crucial. We suggest that wellbeing is a fairly easy concept for all to connect with, and to see the benefit of it. However, a successful strategy is far from simple. Authenticity, leadership, living genuinely and sustainability are all issues that face any organization as they strive to untap what is probably the greatest business benefit out there. The successful strategy is highly dependent on good leadership and effective engagement. As Ann Francke, Chief Executive of the Chartered Management Institute in the UK, so wonderfully put it, 'Leaders who are visible and accessible inspire far more trust than those who are not. Leaders who talk the line – who actively listen to and engage with their middle managers – create far better cultures than those who don't' (Francke, 2017: 5).

Francke went on to detail the importance of authenticity and engagement in management to gain the trust of the workforce. It is only when the relationship between employers is such that true engagement, and to some extent buy-in, starts to feel like reality. As Andy Rhodes, Chief Constable of Lancashire Police, notes, 'wellbeing requires leaders to roll up their sleeves' (Rhodes, 2017). This may seem a little overaggressive, and even incongruent with the overall message, however we have found that getting the message across is no easy feat and is often dependent on difficult conversations being had across the organization. Difficult or 'honest' conversations are unfortunately not the staple of most line management courses, and we argue here that they should be. We can now take a more in-depth look at why.

So, what does an engagement strategy look like? We appreciate that at this point the nuts and bolts of the wellbeing approach may not even be complete, but it is a good juncture to start to consider how it is going to be communicated. If the underlying culture has never before had wellbeing in its midst, then there may well be a lot to do. However, if there is already a proactive HR departmental approach, effective occupational health and a functional L&D then it might be straightforward. Nevertheless, we will assume there is work to be done in each of these areas!

The ingredients required for an effective engagement strategy are largely dependent on existing approaches, what has worked in other areas. We concede that most organizations will, at some point, have undergone a programme of change, in whatever guise. The learning that emerges from any change programme can be the key to getting a wellbeing engagement strategy spot on. Remember, this is good news for the workforce, so should not really be a 'hard sell'. What it should be is a statement to say that the organization takes wellbeing seriously and can clearly see the benefits that it can bring, not only in terms of performance and productivity, but also in the way that employers view and interact with their employees. As we will explore later, this is a compelling vision. It also should not be considered in any way a performance metric as this will really skew what you are trying to do – we will discuss this later in the book.

As previously mentioned, the additional effort our employees are prepared to give to make the organization succeed can be called discretionary or extra-role effort. Or, what you may describe as, 'the amount of work you do when no one is looking!' This is one of the cornerstones of an effective engagement strategy, and something managers will surely note as a sign of success. Trust, clarity, openness and lots of energy are also indicative of getting this and the wider wellbeing strategy right, so could form part of any evaluation you may consider.

Congruent with Seligman's approach (2003, 2011), wellbeing should also be about engaging positively with the workforce, assisting, aiding and developing. It should tie in closely with any leadership approaches or philosophy undertaken. Policies and procedures should also correspond to the messages given. If your organization takes a corporate messaging approach, these too should be in accordance with the wellbeing strategy, cohering and making sense for the workforce. This clarity of purpose, as it is often referred to, can be a powerful means of ensuring organizational commitment, an aspect that alludes many companies.

It should be made clear that engagement in relation to wellbeing is an ongoing process, it is about a mindset. Wellbeing is not simply the absence of ill health, it is much more. Stresses and strains can creep up on workers, not necessarily all emanating from the workplace. Stress can occur through years of what we call the drip-drip-drip effect. That is, it may not be any one significant incident that causes a stressful episode, but a build-up of what, in isolation, may seem a series of innocuous events. However, over time they grow to eventually overwhelm us. This is when our ability to cope, our resilience, is not sufficient for the challenges we are facing.

So, what we are clarifying, and suggesting here, is that engagement is an ongoing effort, and just because it seems that everyone is doing okay on the surface, this does not naturally translate to that being the reality for them. What we are suggesting is that you don't stop engaging in relation to wellbeing, and every contact with employees should involve some element of a wellbeing conversation or enquiry. As John Sutherland so eloquently puts this in his superb TEDx presentation, referring to Edmond Locard's seminal scientific work, 'Every contact leaves a trace' (Sutherland, 2017).

Continued exposure to stressors can lead to depression, anxiety and even suicide. The engagement strategy should therefore look at the long-term interests of employees, and not just those present with ill health. Much of this will depend on the leaders and managers in the workplace. We have already mentioned that these managers may not be as skilled as they ought to be, and these gaps make a good starting point. It is preferable to involve the whole workforce, including part-time, agency and contractors. Remember, it is the *environment* you are trying to influence, and all those in it. We suggest this may even extend to those who have left, for whatever reason, the organization. This leads to employees feeling truly valued by their employers: strong psychological contracts develop and as a result they are prepared to go the extra mile, act on initiative, innovate and invest in their work, keep up to date with professional development and so on. They feel psychologically safe, and well. Engagement is so much more than communicating with employees, or marketing wellbeing; it is about a long-term commitment to the workforce.

Perhaps the most influential work, in our opinion at least, was carried out by David MacLeod and Nita Clarke in their UK work, Engaging for Success. This unpacked just what good engagement looks like in practice. The themes in the subsequent report, which is commonly referred to as the MacLeod report (MacLeod and Clarke, 2009), contain the business case for engagement, the enablers and the barriers, and contain lots of useful references and case studies to illustrate the various points raised. Although we suggest here that the engagement side of things is just one arm of an effective wellbeing approach, it provides a good example of the broader business considerations, pitfalls and performance implications.

We would urge you to read the report, but in essence MacLeod and Clarke suggest that there are four basics that organizations should focus on in order to engage effectively with their employees. These begin with the story of what they are trying, as an organization, to achieve. First, what is it that the company does, or tries to do? Do all the employees, business partners, collaborators, suppliers, customers, and so on, know what this is? It is referred to as the 'strategic narrative', which may help or hinder your interpretation – that is to say, can all involved with the organization provide a short sentence or two that summarizes this? This is a real bonus, as it is fairly easy to test out: go into any department, see people who work for you and simply ask!

Probably the most famous anecdote is provided by the janitor at NASA, who was asked by the visiting President Kennedy what was his role within the organization, and he allegedly replied, 'to put a man on the moon sir'. This also requires your people to have some notion of the organization's history, its present circumstances and its aspirations for the future. Is this clearly communicated, acknowledged and understood? It would be rare for someone to report that they love their job, but not have a clue what the company does! As we have previously mentioned, this links in perfectly to having meaning and purpose in your working life.

A further, and more up to date, example is provided through the eyes of Captain Sully Sullenberger, a US commercial pilot who famously landed a passenger aircraft in the Hudson River, New York, following a bird strike that crippled his jet. All passengers lived in what was popularized as 'the miracle on the Hudson'. In his book, *Making a Difference*, Sully (as he is known) speculated: 'We can have the same training and the same equipment as the competition, but if our workforce takes ownership of the goal and derives something personal and meaningful while achieving it, we will be better and more efficient and perform at a higher level more consistently and more safely' (Sullenberger, 2012: 310).

A final example is provided by a story about Christopher Wren, one of the greatest English architects. One day he was walking, unrecognized, through the men working on the building of St Paul's Cathedral in London, which he designed. 'What are you doing?' he asked one of the workmen. The man replied, 'I'm cutting a piece of stone.' As he walked, he asked the same question to another man, and the man replied, 'I'm earning five shillings two pence a day.'

To a third man he addressed the same inquiry, and the man answered, 'I am helping Sir Christopher Wren build a beautiful cathedral.' That man had vision and was engaged with his work, congruent with our observations on meaning and purpose. He could see beyond the cutting of stone, beyond the earning of his daily wage, to the creation of a work of art, the building of a great cathedral.

Congruent with our earlier observations in this book, MacLeod and Clarke cite their second recommendation on the role of managers, and more specifically the immediate line manager. We have already posited that this role is probably the most critical to wellbeing in the workplace, but what is it they should actually do? This begins with clarifying to those who work with them what success looks like. What are they expected to do, and how will they know when they are doing it well? This is easy to say, but what does this look like, in real life? It is also important that people are treated as individuals. A simple example, and we have seen this a lot especially in big organizations, is that line managers may not even be aware that they are a person's line manager. They may not know the names of the people they are responsible for and, more importantly we suggest, who people are looking to for guidance and advice. This, to some, may seem outrageous, but we can tell you for sure that this exists in many organizations. We also suggest that line managers should be trained, given room, and be encouraged to develop their people in the roles they are performing. They should be empowered, and encouraged, to address dysfunctional or lazy working, with the full support of the organization. These behaviours can be particularly infectious, and other employees who experience their counterparts getting away with such are unlikely to feel motivated and inspired themselves. Effective management is essential, and this is sure to bring, in our opinion, far greater levels of discretionary effort from employees.

The third point made by MacLeod and Clarke is about listening effectively. This is across departments and across teams, however big or small. This is not confined to physical presence – as we alluded to earlier, the Digital Age has brought many platforms with which we can communicate and trust and we note many organizations now have internal communication blogs, discussion forums and so on. Here employee voice can be heard and engaged with, and can be a form of effective listening. Our experience of these internal platforms suggests that executives need to be patient, with nerves of steel on occasion, and let some of these debates play out. Let employees reach some conclusions, or consensus, before joining in or making decisions.

Finally, MacLeod and Clarke suggest that integrity, trust and ethical behaviour is the last bastion of successful engagement. By no means is this an entire compendium of successful engagement, but in terms of employee wellbeing it is fairly difficult to contest. We suggest that organizations who do these things well will almost certainly be great places to work in, and that usually translates into happy employees who draw great meaning and purpose from their work. As we have shown, this directly translates to high levels of productivity, performance and good outcomes for the organization. Staff feel dedicated, focused and display energy. They are advocates for the organization, they perceive it as fair and have a positive, or growth mindset (Syed, 2015). Also, if applicable, customers will report positively on interactions and want to do business with you.

The crux of 'Engage for Success' (Figure 3.2) is in the relationship between employer and employee. These relationships should be positively framed, extending to colleagues, customers and partnerships. The resultant individual and organizational performance improvements that emerge are congruent with the suggestions we make elsewhere within this book. In many ways engagement and wellbeing achieve the same outcomes, both for employers and employees. Conversely, when this is not achieved organizations may experience increases in sickness absenteeism, presenteeism and leaveism. 'Meaningful work leads to lower levels of absence because people are engaged with their work... the association between meaningfulness and engagement is strengthened by wellbeing' (Soane *et al*, 2013).

Figure 3.2   The crux of 'Engage for Success'

We have written extensively about the positive individual outcomes that high levels of psychological wellbeing can bring in terms of being committed to the organization, feeling more positive, having higher morale and generally feeling healthier. Engagement and wellbeing have been described as a virtuous circle and there is a strong correlation between the two.

CASE STUDY   Royal Mail Group UK

This case study is taken from the Post Office services (Royal Mail Group) in the UK, where wellbeing was made one of their strategic priorities (BITC, 2016a). It is a fascinating study in many ways, as the postal services throughout the world have undergone massive transformation. If we look at digitization, and the almost death of sending each other letters, you could be excused for thinking it was all over for the postal services. However, you then see the emergence, ironically, of online platforms such as eBay, which have to some extent remodernized the way we all shop. That is to say, online. This shopping revolution has really led to the reinvention of postal services. What is traditionally a very physical job, having its wellbeing problems in terms of physicality, has also seen an increase in mental health concerns. Let us take a look at how these are being tackled.

Royal Mail Group (UK) worked closely with the Mental Health Foundation in an attempt to understand both their work and their workforce, and how wellbeing could contribute to them becoming, in a clever play on words, 'feeling first class'. Through a series of inputs they aimed to educate their workforce on what the signs of mental health were, what to do about them, how to help colleagues through difficult periods, and what could be done proactively to improve mental wellbeing in the workplace. Set against a backdrop of increasing sickness absence, particularly long-term sickness (2014–15), the company managed to achieve a reduction of more than 100,000 days, making a saving of £12.2 million. They provided educational inputs on how to look after colleagues who were off work sick, including checking in with them, sending them cards, letting them know they are being missed and wishing them well. Small interventions it seems, but these have a huge impact. Generally, the way organizations treat people who are off work ill is not particularly great, and we know that the longer people are off work, the more tenuous these relationships become. It also makes it very difficult to return to the workplace and continue similar relationships to those in existence prior to the period of illness. This is for both physical and mental ill health, but we know for mental ill health this is more pronounced. Other interventions, such as the introduction of trolleys to carry mail, rather than the ubiquitous postman's sack, were also to make life easier for the workforce. The focus on promoting a sustainability mindset amongst the workforce and letting their workers develop has resulted in a change in approach across the company. Internal schemes such as feeling first class, first-class mental health, first-class fitness and first-class diving have been taken incredibly positively by the entire workforce. They ran a pilot of 55 Mental Health First Aid courses for line managers, and have plans to roll this out across the entire organization.

Moya Greene, the then CEO of Royal Mail Group, described the developments as follows: 'Creating a culture where all employees feel able to talk about their wellbeing, and where managers feel empowered to play a role in helping to support those around them, is vital for a competitive and sustainable business. One of the biggest responsibilities lies with leaders, who have a duty to promote the importance of wellbeing right from the very top and ensure that it is recognized as a critical issue by everyone. At Royal Mail, we understand the importance of giving our managers as much support as possible – not only to look after those around them but to ensure they can also maintain positive wellbeing themselves' (BITC, 2016b).

Having provided this example, we now take a look more broadly at training programmes that can help knit together your workplace wellbeing strategy. As we have discussed above, these can have superb outcomes in terms of performance and productivity, but also impact hugely on workplace meaning and purpose.

Training programmes

Having decided on the engagement strategy we now move swiftly on to implementing this with our staff. There is no shortage of providers who have designed a multitude of programmes to address workplace wellbeing. What we suggest here is that first you try to understand what exactly you want to achieve in relation to wellbeing, such as how you wish it to cohere with other business strategies. As Judith Grant and Shaun Davis, the (then) heads of wellbeing at the Royal Mail Group, put into motion, we suggest it becomes a consideration within all decision making to be truly effective. The strategy, if it is to succeed, also needs embedding in the culture of the organization, as Moya Greene mentions above, the way it works, the way employers feel, speak and interact with it. How do employees talk about the organization outside of work? This is a good benchmark. Do they speak fondly, with loyalty and pride, or are they dismissive and undersell it? Having decided how you want it to land, you can then make some choices about training your employees. We suggest you make this explicit, ensuring they know that this is training in wellbeing and that it is an approach that your organization is totally committed to taking. Getting this wrong can have unintended consequences, so it is important that the plan is structured and well thought out. We would also recommend that training is provided top to bottom, throughout the organization, however big or small. Some of the key components to any training input are included as follows, although we concede this is not an exhaustive list.

Primarily, as previously mentioned in the 'Engage for Success' work by MacLeod and Clarke, there needs to be executive buy-in to any training programmes. The support, as clearly given by the previous Royal Mail Group example, of the CEO (or equivalent) is essential. Without this the workforce may never feel fully supported in their efforts. It is good practice for any training inputs to begin with making that support explicit. If that is in person, fantastic, but we live in a modern age whereby other means can be employed if the gold standard is out of reach. Second, it is vital that all in the organization are aware that programmes exist and can be accessed. As mentioned previously with metrics, if this is a competition it is unlikely to achieve its desired outcomes. We will talk more about competition in the workplace in the next chapter, but when it comes to wellbeing this rarely bares fruit.

Training providers

A big concern with wellbeing training is the delivery agent. This can be contentious and to a large extent budget bound. What we would suggest is that getting one of your employees who is recuperating from stress doing wellbeing inputs is not perhaps the best way forward. Now some may scoff at this, but we have seen this time and time again in organizations, and all manner of problems can arise if this is your plan. Wellbeing needs to be delivered by people who are passionate and truly believe in the merits of what they are saying. Although external providers can seem expensive, it may be worth the investment in the long term. We have experience in the delivery of resilience training and the efficacy of such in the workplace, and have seen first-hand the fantastic impact that a professional input can have on a team, especially in the long term.

CASE STUDY UK Police Force

A great example for this chapter is illustrated in the one-day resilience workshops delivered by Robertson Cooper Limited to police employees in the UK. These resilience workshops took both police officers and police staff on a journey around how they thought about things, how they processed them and how they adapted, coped and responded. Having confidence is important, especially in such an occupation, in order to do your job with a positive mindset and ensuring those you are working with also feel that way. The course also explored social support and building good relationships. Sometimes that was not easy outside the occupation, with issues of confidentiality and trust playing a large role. Another area the course addressed was that of having a clear sense of purpose, and not letting that reduce during a career by normalizing difficult encounters, upset and torment. The final area was that of flexibility and adaptability, noting that some work was unclear, unexpected and sometimes quite daunting. The results from this course were striking. Our research showed significantly better results in terms of stressors in the workplace in people who had undertaken this course of training.

Many others provide inputs on this topic, and we would suggest some research is carried out to satisfy yourself that it will actually prove worthwhile in your own particular context. For example, has the training you are considering been independently evaluated? If so, who by? Like any other area of business, significant investment in your people requires careful consideration. To keep a thread of consistency, and congruent with our descriptions of the four areas of wellbeing, we suggest inputs follow the same path. Let us look at these now.

Course content

The all-important question now is what to include in any training programmes you are considering. Again, as previously mentioned this is largely down to what your organization does, or the service it provides. In some respects, what we are looking for is best fit in terms of the working context. We acknowledge that these will include differing settings, people and needs. However, what we can offer, based on the fundamentals of what impacts in the workplace, is a ball-park illustration of good practice, including the following elements, and it is down to your organization to prioritize these. It may be that you prefer to focus on particular elements, dependent on what the perceived issues are in the workplace. Once again, we reiterate that these may be just that, perceptions, and may have no resemblance with reality at all. You may also prioritize based on forthcoming change programmes, sickness absence trends, pay structures, or inter-departmental relationship problems. These are more than likely to be covered within these four recommendations, as outlined in Figure 3.3.

Figure 3.3 Recommended focus of wellbeing training inputs

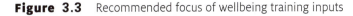

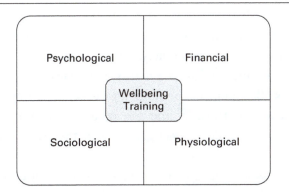

A traditional view of wellbeing has been to watch your weight (BMI), watch what you eat, don't drink too much alcohol, avoid certain foods, embrace certain foods, get plenty of sleep, exercise regularly, take regular holidays, enjoy time with your family, don't do drugs and so on. Although all this is great advice, we feel it is a little too basic to form any sort of meaningful strategy for an organization. This is especially pertinent when you consider that most organizations have very little control over any of these aspects of an employee's life. So, let us now look in a little more depth about what each of these aspects may look like in the form of an organizational wellbeing input. Furthermore, what can organizations do to promote and have their workforce engage with the key messages each area involves? These can have a big impact on your workforce, so are worthy of consideration, although we appreciate it may not be feasible to implement all. As we have mentioned previously though, it is unlikely that any of these will impact your people in isolation, and you may find it is very much a domino effect. For example, people who run into financial difficulties may find they have to cut back on going out (societal impact), cutting back on leisure or gym memberships (physical impact), which may then lead them to feel withdrawn or slightly depressed (psychological impact). There are numerous combinations that can conspire to result in sub-optimal wellbeing. Starting with any one of the four, you can soon join together a series of events that result in all aspects joining in. A brief footnote, financial wellbeing does not, as you will not be surprised to hear, equate to all the rest being okay. In other words, being wealthy does not, of course, automatically mean you are healthy. It seems that quite the opposite can occur in actual fact, with many millionaires and billionaires reporting being depressed, feeling isolated and lonely. We know that many of us would like to have a 'quick go' to see if this is actually true, but research suggests it is! Bringing this analogy into a work setting, it does not always follow that those at the top of an organization – the big earners or power holders – feel great about themselves or that they don't have wellbeing flaws. Our concerns about wellbeing are just as pertinent across the entire workforce, whatever position you occupy.

Psychological

We will start with what we consider the most impactive and most difficult area of wellbeing to get right in the workplace. For every element of our being has a psychological dimension and, as such, this is a critical area of workplace strategy. We have already explored some of the dynamics at play with how an employee interacts with the workplace, whether that be an actual working office or factory, or other work space. But, we now have a growing degree of home, virtual, remote working options and these can prove extremely tricky to supervise as well as work in. What we often see are workers putting huge amounts of hours in when they work remotely, as if to prove they are not shirking. Likewise, and sometimes polar, employees in offices seem to spend their day putting in, well, facetime. We are talking facetime in terms of presenteeism here, rather than the popular social media app!

Our suggestions in this area would be to begin by looking at how employees interact with the workplace, what they draw from it. Meaning and purpose, and we realize we keep stressing this, but it is so important, is the key here. One way to explore this is to explore self-awareness, positivity, empathy and notions of caring for each other. How do we define these aspects and relate them to working life? How do employees relate to each other in the workplace, show solidarity, work to a common goal and have a real drive to work as a collective? As we discussed earlier, gaming is very rarely sustainably productive, so effectively promoting competition amongst a workforce who work with each other for long periods of time is not going to prove good for the psychological wellbeing of the workforce.

Therefore, we suggest that a little bit of context setting takes place, along with the analyses as to where you wish to get to. Mental health first aid, psychological safety, behavioural risk management and other such courses of learning can help your organization get set to prepare and address issues as and when they arrive. What is more, your people will feel valued, cared for, and more committed to the organization. This is another area to consider, in that you need to decide what you are going to do on an organizational level, a team level and of course individually. Is your approach reactive or proactive, and how near are you going to sail to the medical world? This can be a source of confusion when designing and implementing your wellbeing strategy, so it is best to be clear about where you intend it to sit on the health continuum.

One of the major differences with psychological (or mental) health is that it is sometimes not as easy to spot as other areas. For example, if one of your employees suddenly starts to limp, it is a fair assumption that they have sustained an injury to a lower limb. You can probably even guess which limb or, with a little more analysis, even whereabouts in the leg. However, what do we look for with mental ill health? Inputs that cover this can often prove insightful, but of course there are caveats, as with most things. So, for example, if people are distressed (the opposite to 'eustress', which as we have already discussed, is 'good' stress) there are a number of things that may change in terms of their appearance, such as being unusually untidy. They may not be washing or ironing their clothes, or they might wear the same clothes for days and days. They might be agitated, moody, irritable, or excessively (for them of course) laid back, lethargic or disinterested. There are many things to look out for, and we consider such inputs can be of real value – as is doing something about it, helping them in other words. This too can also be a minefield, with a number of different approaches available. For example, are you considering self-help, providing information, sign-posting services, in-house provision, outsourcing, employee assistance programmes, dedicated help lines, one-to-one counselling services, IT service provision – the list is endless. We conclude this piece on psychological health by saying there is a lot of help and support available, and doing nothing in your organization should not be one of the options.

Financial

This is often overlooked due to it most likely being the most distant from the medical world. However, money worries can be debilitating. They almost always lead to manifestations in the other three areas of psychological, sociological and physiological wellbeing, and can also be the result of problems arising in the other areas, so it is important that financial health is given some thought in any training that is given to employees. We would suggest, in the light of the 'gig' economy that is being mooted, that this is now more relevant than ever. Financial education sessions can be worked in to the other areas, or be threaded through as considerations quite easily. You can view financial wellbeing through a similar lens, financial screening, protecting yourself and your family. Screening involves looking at the viability of your outgoings in respect of incoming monies. In simple terms, does it add up? Just like the other areas we suggest, it is better to be a proactive activity rather than a reactive one! This may include any debt consolidation or reducing activity you have undertaken if you are not enjoying financial health (outgoings are more than your income). Themes like lifestyle, big investments such as mortgages and car purchase can have a huge impact on a person's life, and ought to be planned carefully. We also recommend, as with the other areas, that you seek some expert advice on this if you can.

As we have previously mentioned, in terms of wellbeing the challenges don't usually come in isolation and financial worries often provide the trigger for a number of reactions. For example, we may take on work that whilst it is of no interest to us really, will help pay the bills and keep our families in comfort. This can often cause mixed feelings, or as Steve Peters puts it in his iconic book *The Chimp Paradox*

(2012), disturb our inner chimp! The opposite may be felt if we are doing work we really enjoy, but it is not earning us enough money to live on. This could be likened to the time we spend looking after dependants, where the time consumed is such that we could be earning money. Of course, this touches on us psychologically, but the initial trigger may be financial and therefore is worthy of consideration here.

A further area one may wish to explore might be the notion that money does not bring you happiness. If ever there was a contested statement to stir the grey matter, this is it. What research seems to indicate is that extreme wealth, say in the top quartile, may well cause more problems than it is worth. Take, for example, the endless reporting on wealthy celebrities suffering stress, anxiety and depression. It seems that no amount of Mercedes or Chihuahuas can stifle these psychological stressors, proving the point to some extent! We make light of this, but of course it is a serious issue, and again highlights the curse of financial wellbeing, as some may view it. What we may conclude here is that you cannot solve wellbeing issues by throwing more money at people.

CASE STUDY   Antonio Horto-Osario, Lloyds Bank, and Elon Musk, SpaceX and Tesla

By way of example the Chief Executive of Lloyds Bank, Antonio Horto-Osario, described his own battle with mental ill health in a magazine interview for *The Times*. In the interview he described how stress left him almost unable to function, describing his experience as comparable with torture. Horto-Osario went on to describe how he now works to end the stigma of workplace stress (Carpenter, 2017). In respect of our point here, this is from a man who earnt a staggering US $10.3 million in 2016. Further examples of meaning and purpose over financial reward are to be found in the story of Elon Musk, of SpaceX and Tesla fame. As one of the richest men on the planet, Musk is consumed largely with his quest to colonize further planets and run the Earth on a more sustainable footing (Vance, 2016). His ambition to produce the largest battery was realized in late 2017, as the battery went online in Australia. It is capable of powering some 30,000 homes and is the size of an American football field (although Musk is originally from South Africa).

Sociological

Again, ignore this aspect at your peril. If work is the only focus in your life, and you put your heart and soul into it, even when on days off, you are eventually going to find yourself in bother. It is critical to your wellbeing to have time away from the workplace, socializing with friends and loved ones. Having an interest, hobby or leisure pursuit outside of what may be considered work will pay dividends in the long run. Often social groups stem from the workplace, or are initiated via workplace schemes and this is fine as long as the result does not end up work related. So, sports and social clubs, work outings, work-sponsored gym memberships or leisure activities are all fine. We would recommend this forms part of your work, effectively 'giving back' to you reward for your efforts. This can be a powerful way of cementing the psychological contract you have with work also, but is definitely not work dependent.

Encouraging employees, as part of your workplace wellbeing offering, to engage in activities outside work on a regular basis may appear at first glance somewhat counter-productive. However, we consider this a must for any employer that has their long-term sustainability front and centre in workplace planning. Many organizations also view this as part of their corporate social responsibility. A happy workforce with high levels of meaning and purpose are surely going to be more productive, have better-quality contact with customers and stakeholders, and all-round perform better. To a certain extent, internal company events can initiate this feeling of belonging by effectively rewarding behaviours and celebrating success.

Physiological

When we talk about wellbeing, the common descriptions often focus on physiological. Keeping physically well is probably the easiest of our quartet to understand and execute, although the best ways are often contentious. What is too much or too little? How much time should you spend every day, and so on.

We also have the, relatively recent, introduction of wearable tech to help with our quest. This can be in terms of individuals, or team challenges such as the Global Fitness Challenge. This involves work teams doing set numbers of steps per day, working up to 10,000 with a view to keeping physically active. With modern work types being largely computer based, the sedentary behaviours that accompany this can be very bad for our health. Information about this particular element of wellbeing is available in abundance, so we will just mention one or two of the basics here.

One of the many challenges workers face is how to balance physical fitness with the demands of modern working life and family commitments. Then there are the additional challenges that the ageing body throws up. This is not easy, and we suggest the art lies in trying to combine exercise with your daily activities. Options such as taking the stairs for at least some of your journey, rather than a lift. Walking some of the way to work, maybe purposefully parking that little bit further away. All these take effort, and during what can be a challenging working day it may be the last thing on your mind. However, these can all help, and setting the tone in the workplace can be a great way of promoting exercise.

As we have mentioned, there is an abundance of information out there, so we recommend that consideration is given to taking a good look at what is available before working physiological considerations into your strategy. Good organizations seem to do this really well, with after-work classes, sports leagues within work and other such initiatives. However, if you work for a small company this may not be practicable, so you may have to look at a further means of delivering on this aspect.

Physiological aspects often get dragged into the healthy lifestyle debate as well – diet and exercise, as it is often abbreviated. However, these are just one part of a complexity of facets that need to be considered when deciding what is a healthy lifestyle.

Summary

In summary, all these aspects need to be considered when looking at what you are going to offer, what we have termed course content. So, the common notions of diet and exercise are important, but so too are stress reduction, correct amounts of sleep, work–life balance, having a suitable working environment, having a good boss, being a good boss. Taking care of your financial situation and living within your means can also contribute significantly to your wellness. Finally, having a good social circle, having time away from the workplace with friends and family, having a hobby or enjoying a sport – these societal wellbeing aspects are so important. Having taken all this on board, our next chapter looks at common errors when approaching wellbeing, and how you might be able to overcome or mitigate against these.

Key takeaways from this chapter

Strategy setting

We cannot emphasize enough the importance of this – effectively this is the essence of this book. At the heart of a wellbeing strategy is positivity, meaning and purpose. Without these we have just words on a page. Once set, the strategy must dovetail with existing strategies and be seen as both realistic and achievable by all those it will impact upon. It should be viewed with pride by the organization and championed as a major asset to the business.

Goals

These are what you are setting out to achieve in terms of your wellbeing strategy, and they must be realistic and achievable, as should your overall strategy. Make sure the goals are clearly defined and communicated effectively to ensure your people are aware of what it is you want to achieve.

Personal resilience

Broadly speaking there are two aspects to personal resilience. The ability to cope with everyday life, the drip-drip-drip, is the first. The second is the ability, or having enough in reserve, to be able to deal with a major traumatic event that impacts heavily on you. High levels of personal resilience can be a life-saver. It can also be learnt, improved and controlled in a number of ways, as per our discussion on resilience training.

Stress

Stress has been called the health epidemic of the 21st century and is normally associated with ill health. However, some stress can be good for us – eustress being the good part, distress being the bad. The important point is to know that in reaction to stressors the body releases all sorts of chemicals, and realizing what is happening can help us to understand the importance of keeping ourselves within our coping zones.

Trauma

Probably better known through its part in post-traumatic stress disorder (PTSD), trauma exposure can be debilitating and should be taken very seriously, especially if this is something our workers are expected to deal with. Thankfully not all occupations involve trauma exposure, but for those that do, such as emergency service workers, it is important to know what to look out for and how to help. Trauma exposure very often requires expert intervention.

The Resilience Prescription

This is a widely used set of aspects that are known to impact on our stress levels and ability to cope. Some knowledge of these elements may help you understand the impact factors on both yourself and your colleagues, as well as their options for coping.

Wellbeing and engagement

These two areas really go hand in glove. Engagement is so important when considering wellbeing. We refer to a number of key authors on engagement as well as a case study to illustrate the point here. Engagement can bring great rewards if done correctly and highlights the criticality of effectively communicating with, and listening to, your people.

Training programmes

We try not to fall into the trap of suggesting everything requires more training. However, existing programmes need to incorporate elements of wellbeing in their syllabus. They should also not suggest incongruent approaches that threaten or decrease the opportunities to thrive in the workplace. We also suggest any training programmes that are delivered are evaluated and, if possible, independently.

Course content

It is critical that training programmes adequately deal with the key issues of wellbeing. We consider these to be the physiological, sociological, psychological and financial aspects of wellbeing. These, of course, can be broken down into a number of sub-elements. However, the constructs reflect the need to concentrate efforts on the working environment, how leaders interact with the workforce and aspects of personal resilience.

References

Balogun, J (2007) The practice of organizational restructuring: From design to reality, *European Management Journal*, **25** (2), pp 81–91

BITC (2016a) [accessed 4 August 2018] Royal Mail Group – Feeling First Class [Online] https://www.bitc.org.uk/resources-training/case-studies/royal-mail-group-feeling-first-class

BITC (2016b) [accessed 4 August 2018] Leading on Mental Wellbeing – Transforming the Role of Line Managers: A Blueprint for Unlocking Employee Mental Wellbeing and Productivity [Online] https://wellbeing.bitc.org.uk/system/files/research/bitc_linemanagerreport_feb2016_final.pdf

Carpenter, L (2017) [accessed 4 August 2018] The CEO of Lloyds Bank Turned its Fortunes Around – But the Anxiety Almost Broke Him, *The*

Times, 7 October [Online] https://www.thetimes.co.uk/article/the-ceo-of-lloyds-bank-turned-its-fortunes-around-but-the-anxiety-almost-broke-him-fg970cpjr

Francke, A (2017) Walk and talk: your management must-dos, *Professional Manager*, Chartered Management Institute

Johnson, G, Scholes, K and Whittington, R (2008) *Exploring Corporate Strategy*, 8th edn, Pearson Education, London

Kandel, E (2017) [accessed 4 August 2018] Identical Twins – Not Identical Brains: Cold Spring Harbor Laboratory [Online] https://www.dnalc.org/view/1200-Identical-Twins-Not-Identical-Brains.html

MacLeod, D and Clarke, N (2009) [accessed 4 August 2018] Engaging For Success: Enhancing Performance Through Employee Engagement, *Department for Business Innovation and Skills* [Online] http://www.engageforsuccess.org/wp-content/uploads/2012/09/file52215.pdf

Mintzberg, H (2009) Rebuilding companies as communities, *Harvard Business Review*, 87 (7, 8), pp 140–43

Peters, S (2012) *The Chimp Paradox*, Vermilion, London

Porter, M and Kramer, R (2002) The competitive advantage of corporate philanthropy, *Harvard Business Review*, December

Rhodes, A (2017) Speech at the Excellence in Policing Conference, Ryton, UK

Robertson, I, Cooper, C, Sarkar, M and Curran, T (2015) Resilience training in the workplace from 2003 to 2014: a systematic review, *Journal of Occupational Psychology*, 88 (3), pp 533–62

Seligman, M (2003) *Authentic Happiness: Using the new positive psychology to realize your potential for deep fulfillment*, Nicholas Brealey, London

Seligman, M (2011) *Flourish: A new understanding of happiness and well-being – and how to achieve them*, Nicholas Brealey, London

Selye (1975) Confusion and controversy in the stress field, *Journal of Human Stress*, 1 (2), pp 37–44

Soane, E, Shantz, A, Alfes, K, Truss, C, Rees, C and Gatenby, M (2013) The association of meaningfulness, wellbeing, and engagement with absenteeism: A moderated mediation model, *Human Resource Management*, 52 (3), pp 441–56

Southwick, S and Charney, D (2012) *Resilience: The science of mastering life's greatest challenges*, Cambridge University Press, New York

Sullenberger, C (2012) *Making a Difference: Stories of vision and courage from America's leaders*, Harper Collins Publishers, New York

Sutherland, J (2017) [accessed 1 August 2018] Every Contact Leaves a Trace, *TEDx* [Online] https://www.youtube.com/watch?v=ibl3M4dTF2U

Syed, M (2015) *Black Box Thinking: Why most people never learn from their mistakes – but some do*, John Murray, London

Vance, A (2016) *Elon Musk: How the billionaire CEO of SpaceX and Tesla is shaping our future*, HarperCollins, New York

Problems
and pitfalls

04

Introduction

An important aspect to consider in any wellbeing strategy in the workplace is what you can reasonably expect to be simple to implement, and what may not be. In order to do this, it is important to highlight the potential problems and pitfalls of implementing a wellbeing strategy and how to avoid these. We will later explain how to monitor, measure and evaluate a wellbeing strategy, including information on what to measure, how frequently to measure and how to analyse the data. First, we will focus on how to avoid some common mistakes when implementing approaches to better the wellbeing of your workforce. Not only can such mistakes be costly, and potentially embarrassing, but they will also threaten the psychological contract an employee can have with their employers. An internet search will reveal the cost of sickness absenteeism, both in relation to direct and indirect costs. These are significant, and we hope that this book will provide you with the tools and techniques to make substantial gains in respect of these costs.

Having employees away from the workplace due to sickness is inevitable. However, research has shown time and time again that a lot of this is wholly preventable. Though we concede not all. An effective wellbeing strategy, implemented well and evaluated, can prove highly valuable. It also leads to a strong bond forming with the workforce, one in which they feel understood, valued and part of the organization; we have spoken of identity throughout this book.

Focus

When we are asked to describe wellbeing, it can be fairly difficult to do, as it means so many things to so many people. What we usually begin with is what this means in terms of the particular organization in which it is set. People often describe wellbeing in physical terms: 'get plenty of exercise, eat the right foods, don't drink too much, don't smoke, the importance of getting enough sleep' and so on. Unfortunately, however, this narrative describes but a small piece of the wellbeing construct and may be one that most of us have some ideas around controlling and regulating. What is not so obvious, perhaps, is the impact that financial wellbeing, psychological wellbeing and societal wellbeing have on us as human beings. These are often the areas that 'catch us out' and we would suggest that three facets combine to have the most impact on our wellbeing as a whole – these are leadership, resilience and creating the right environment for us to successfully experience meaning and purpose in our working life.

One of the issues for those charged with the responsibility of creating and maintaining the wellbeing strategy is the sheer amount of areas that you can focus on. As wellbeing becomes ever more popular, and the links with performance and productivity in an uber-competitive world become clearer by the day, it is not difficult to realize why this might be so. One of the pitfalls might be trying/attempting to look from every angle. Like anything, a thin coating on the surface may seem okay at the outset, but very often may fail if it is not underpinned by robust evidence. There is also an eye-watering number of options and products on the market to assist you (this book is one of them also!). Untangling these can be difficult, but is well worth it. We have touched on four areas earlier in this book: physical, psychological, financial and societal wellbeing. These can form the basis of your approach, but you will need to then be a little more specific in defining what areas to look at as sub-sections of these areas. So, for example, in terms of societal wellbeing you may wish to look at relationships, friendship circles, trust, community, clubs, events, teamwork and so on. Each of these may also involve a number of areas to look at. These, as could the other areas, may also include broader topics such as politics, equality, education, ethics. All these potentially have an impact on the wellbeing of the workforce.

The focus when considering strategic direction should, in part, be borne out of the engagement with the workforce. Feeling a sense of contribution is critical if wellbeing plans are to succeed. We will look at the impact of culture a little later in the chapter, and how this can have an enormous weighting. For now, though, we will remain with focus. Allowing the wellbeing plan to wander can have unfavourable consequences, but you may wish to balance this with remaining with a little flexibility in the system. This allows you room to react to changes in the workplace, such as having extra work, having less work, having different work, or legislative changes. These may require you to instigate small changes to take account of the emergent circumstances. These subtleties allow organizations to lead the way, and being efficient at taking the workforce on the journey is one of the many benefits that a focus on wellbeing will yield. As with the rest of the book, what we are suggesting here are actions that will bring both business success and a happy workforce that has meaning and purpose, integral to their working life.

Mindset

A fairly recent phenomenon, mindset refers to the notions, assumptions or values held by a person or group of people – a world view, if you wish. The particular interpretations we are most interested in were coined by Carol Dweck, who categorized mindsets as either fixed or growth (2006). She proposed that people deal with failures in two distinct ways. Those with a fixed mindset view failure as an inability to operate at the required level. Those with a growth mindset believe one can acquire or learn the necessary skills to function at the required level. Dweck's research suggests that adopting a growth mindset can help with your own personal resilience, happiness and performance. The notion that people are malleable and can grow and develop is the underpinning philosophy of the approach.

Although hindsight is a great thing, it is rarely that statements such as 'should of', 'could of', 'why didn't they' and 'would of' are helpful. To have a growth mindset, as Matthew Syed suggests in his wonderful book *Black Box Thinking* (Syed, 2015), one needs to look at what is helpful in the scenario presented. Ideally, proactivity is preferable to reactivity. That is to say, if we get wellbeing right up front, there should be limited necessity to turn to a review of what went wrong. Even if this is the reality, as it inevitably will be on occasion, then how you proceed next will say a lot about how right you have got wellbeing in your organization. For example, are you looking to what went wrong and who is to blame, or are you seeking to establish if there is any learning or future developments that can stop this happening to anyone else? If someone is grossly negligent of course, or criminally oriented, then sanction may be inevitable. However, this is rarely helpful and effectively sets your overall aim back as your people recover from whatever has happened. We suggest that, on occasion, these opportunities to learn often advance the wellbeing agenda – and on occasion, quite significantly! That is, learning by our mistakes. A large amount of the work carried out by Dweck was conducted in an educational environment, examining learning and classroom performance. Like Syed, she argued that the characteristics of a growth mindset can be learnt over time, and applied incrementally – what Syed referred to as marginal gains, in his case to improve performance when competition is tight.

We therefore conclude that having a growth mindset is a key component to practitioners involved in promoting workplace wellbeing. It is a very helpful trait, is positively focused and developmental in nature. On the other hand, a fixed mindset leaves little room for manoeuvre, is process driven, negative or neutral in nature and seeks to apportion blame rather than learn from errs.

Management by metrics

'If you can measure it, you can manage it', so the saying goes. We couldn't agree less with this statement, and we will discuss here the enormous psychological damage on the workforce that narrow-minded thinking about metrics management has brought about.

What is more, there is still a whole generation in the workplace, actively managing good people, as we speak, who know no other way of managing than to rely on this archaic dysfunctional approach to people. When we look at management trends (or fads as they are often termed) over the years, some of these have been less than helpful in terms of the wellbeing agenda. Take, for example, the damning impact of data-driven leadership in various organizations that took hold in the 1990s. People were being judged by the notion of how much, how often, how many, what percentage, and so on. This focus on output rather than outcome has been most damaging, especially to the psyche of the human people fleet. As if that wasn't sufficient, they were then judged using these same metrics against their work colleagues, very often in their own teams, as if this was some sort of management utopia.

Unfortunately, there were lots of managers promoted on their ability to put into practice these very damaging ways of leading, and some now occupy executive positions in organizations. So, there is a warning if this hasn't quite weaned its way out of your own organization yet! The tenets of wellbeing rarely accord to any of what was ironically termed, 'new public management' (Hood, 1991). Chapter 5 will look at monitoring, measuring and evaluating wellbeing, so we are not saying this is a total no-no. What we are saying, however, is that this aspect is fraught with dangers. These can include perceived contradictions and misplaced performance metrics. To provide an example:

CASE STUDY   UK Police Force

The police in the UK, like many other organizations, took advantage of leaps in technological capabilities at the turn of the 21st century. The ability to input all sorts of data on crimes, offenders, locations, resources available, calls for service, and so on, saw the whole service change dramatically. These changes, in the name of efficiency, meant that officers and staff could be deployed, managed, assessed and rewarded on the output from a computer. The problem is, of course, that policing is a non-binary function. With the majority of incidents there is no set process, and the ability to resolve issues is based, largely, on a human being's knowledge and experience in resolving complex personal issues. When managers withdraw the ability to use that discretion there are a number of subsequent results. The most critical of these results is that officers and staff experience reductions in their meaning and purpose; their wellbeing. Further unintended consequences are that those leading in such a way are rewarded by promoting more of their own behaviour in the workforce. Their success is judged on their ability to interpret data and sweat assets (people) in some perverse notion that this provides public value for money. As this era comes to an end, with a new breed of 'people leaders' the trail of destruction is evident to all, with large numbers of officers retired on ill-health grounds, reports of low morale, and a crisis in recruitment of high-calibre officers and staff. These toxic workplaces did nothing to promote the profession and cultural tales of performance by metric still pervade today.

So, if your wellbeing strategy has metrics, by which you monitor, evaluate, measure or gauge success, we urge great care is taken in just how you go about this. Whilst we concede it is necessary, especially to monitor efficacy, how employees perceive this is critical. For if your employees see this as some sort of performance indicator, league table or such, you may actually be doing more harm than good. Simon Guilfoyle wrote passionately about the dark art of performance in his book on systems thinking (Guilfoyle, 2013). In this Guilfoyle suggests, in the context of policing in the UK, that much of the data mined does not actually serve much of a purpose. But perhaps even more damning is what he terms as the unintended consequences this brings about. Resonating with Matthew Syed's accounts in *Black Box Thinking* (Syed, 2015), Guilfoyle suggests that having targets and league tables sets about a chain of events that causes conflict, friction, distrust and other unsavoury phenomena in the workplace, none of which is congruent with a genuine approach to wellbeing. So, if you consider that pitting one employee against another is the way to go, then wellbeing is probably not your first choice. However, we hope that this book may go some way to influence you that if actually the performance or productivity in an organization is your raison d'être, then wellbeing is the way to go in any case. It is also sustainable and, of course, humane!

Sporting analogy

A further potential pitfall is to compare your organization with that of the quest of an elite athlete. So, if your organization is involved with the training of elite athletes please feel free to skip this next couple of paragraphs. However, if it is not, we wish to highlight one or two inconsistencies between, for example, running the 1500 metre at the Beijing Olympics and, say, working as a plumber in a small rural town. We do seem attracted to stories of overcoming the odds, pushing beyond the limits, being the best of the best, and so on. However, if you are trying to, let's say, run a hospital ward, or a team of engineers, these sorts of narratives can be unhelpful. What you require is not 'max-nursing' or 'extreme engineering' – what you are after is very often precision, reliability and, to some extent, a quality of service to your customers. What elite sports folk do have in bucket loads is the ability to concentrate on themselves and their training regime – at all costs. Now, here we are not critiquing this approach, but it is hardly the same as working for five years at Marks & Spencer retail outlet. Here, what may be required, in bucket loads, is good teamwork, reliability, loyalty to the company and a good work ethic.

Athletes, let's say Olympians, are constantly training to be the best they can be at some date in the future. Everything they do is with a view to a couple of dates in peak shape for this event, and thus requires a very different approach and, we would suggest, management. Although the world of motivational speaking can be, well, very motivational, an Olympic gold medallist addressing your nightshift is probably going to do not much more than instil in them that, well, they have probably not achieved quite as much as they had hoped. Is this good for their wellbeing in the long term? What we are suggesting here, albeit tongue-in-cheek, is that wellbeing needs to be sited in reality for your employees as much as it possibly can. Although it is nice to rub shoulders with the celebrity set, the messaging that underpins can deflate. A great deal can be gained from employees' feelings of worth, having meaning and purpose, and feeling like they are succeeding in work – and life.

We can compare a few traits to help illustrate this point more clearly. For example, if we look at training, in sport it is not uncommon for 90 per cent of a competitor's time to be spent training for the event to be competed in. In work, we spend about 10 per cent training (rightly or wrongly) and 90 per cent performing our work itself (what we get paid for). Furthermore, in sport, tiny increases in performance make a huge difference, whereas in work small differences in individual performance are normally relatively trivial. As we will see in the next chapter, measuring performance in sport is relatively easy. It is very often set up just to achieve this (measuring one against another using whatever method to serve the competition). In a work environment, this is more intricate and complex.

Flow

There are, however, one or two helpful comparisons in a working environment, and one of those is to be found in 'being in the zone'. Like sportsmen and women, some of our peak performance at work is delivered when we are 'in the zone'. With origins in mindfulness, this is when we manage to concentrate at our highest levels. This is usually achieved somewhere quiet, and is definitely achieved uninterrupted. One of the characteristics about this intense work zone is that time will fly by, you may have little idea of the passage of time as you become immersed and transfixed with work. This can be immensely satisfying, is often very productive, and brings about an inner peace that those experiencing it often enjoy. Mihaly Csikszentmihalyi (1992) called this being in 'flow', which is a term that has been used by Martin Seligman also as a descriptor of engagement (2011) – flow relating to the optimal psychological experience to bring about high productivity or performance. In sporting terms, this is often seen as athletes prepare to take on that all-important penalty shot, or a moment requiring huge concentration levels, where they seem to close down all other external stimuli. Csikszentmihalyi suggested this could be utilized by individuals to achieve subjective wellbeing (happiness), when they are in the optimal state of intrinsic motivation, fully immersed, at one, and those sorts of conceptions. He suggested eight components to produce flow, in turn to create happiness.

These conditions are:

1 That the goals are clear and not conflicting with other activities.

2 That feedback is clear, immediate and useful.

3 That the challenge is appropriate to the skills and abilities of the person doing it. These are in balance, achievable, capable of being enjoyable. These cannot be boring, too mundane or challenging.

4 That you are focused, concentrating on what you are doing. This brings you into being in the moment.

5 That the person enters a state of becoming oblivious to other things around them.

6 Feeling in control over what is going on, and your part in that process.

7 The loss of self-consciousness.

8 That the passage of time stands still – you have been so engrossed in the activity that time has flown by.

There are a number of books on this subject that are fascinating reads, when you might, in fact, experience flow! As with sports, a lot of the underpinnings are concerned with motivation, so although we largely downplay the use of sporting analogy in everyday 'normal' working life here, there are limited uses, as long as medals are not the end goal!

Culture

We probably could not get away without saying something meaningful about wellbeing and that old academic battleground of culture. There are two main views of organizational culture: 1) sociological, that is, that organizations *have* cultures, and 2) anthropological, that organizations *are* the culture. Most seem to agree that the concept refers to a social construction, the informal norms, values, attitudes, taken-for-granted assumptions and practices by people in an organization. Some may prefer the word 'climate', but really it matters not what we call it but what it does and the power it wields in relation to wellbeing.

Culture, some may say whether positively or negatively, influences a lot of what we do, say, and the opinions, attitudes and perceptions we hold; therefore, it is a big deal. Some may say that everything in an organization can be the culture and therefore, when designing and implementing a wellbeing strategy, ignore it at your peril! In relation to the workplace, culture is often dominated by concern, or fear about speaking out, voicing your opinion, making suggestions, being critical, constructive and other suchlike behaviours.

CASE STUDY   Sexual harassment in Westminster and the film industry

During 2017 there were two examples that shed light on the sheer power of culture in organizations. One involved UK members of parliament and their behaviour towards others, largely subordinates. In this case a sexual harassment scandal, widely reported, swept through the seat of government in Westminster. Although the prime minister intervened, eventually, it was after a lot of damage had been done to many individuals, including some subsequently taking their own lives (Collingridge, Shipman and Pogrund, 2017). What had clearly prevailed was a strong culture where somehow this was seemingly acceptable. The prime minister called for, 'a new culture of respect' (Wright, 2017). However, it begs the question as to why people do not speak up about wrongdoings. The answer, it seems, is that it is not within the culture of the organization, the operating paradigm. Furthermore, to change this paradigm seems to be well beyond issuing a parliamentary decree.

The second example, which was reported globally, was of sexual harassment in the film industry. Powerful producers, directors, lead actors and so on were exposed to all manner of despicable behaviours. This led to a storm of controversy, yet for many years had gone unchallenged, it having been culturally acceptable in order to get on in the industry. Whilst, retrospectively, this seems astonishing, what this next section will explain is why it might happen. It might be an interesting exercise to see if you can track what is going on with these case examples as you read the next section.

Wellbeing, as we have already mentioned, depends on buy-in, commitment and a general respect and regard for people in the workplace. Sometimes these are not well received. If this is so, then that is probably something to do with the culture existent in the organizational setting. Now the really tricky part to this is that wellbeing does not feel at home in such an environment. As we have mentioned several times already in this book, quite the opposite is where wellbeing would thrive, rather than survive. That is, a working environment where wellbeing is wholly accepted and people seek to make improvements in the workplace, rather than wellbeing being just another tick in the box that workers respect but do not really buy in to. Understanding the forces of culture, being able to explain the components and how they act, can be of huge benefit.

One of the good things about culture is that there are now a plethora of ways to both spot it, and influence it. Cultural questionnaires, workshops, audits and suchlike can all help if you are finding that your wellbeing approach is, well, just not landing as you had hoped.

Cultural Web

One of the most helpful ways to take a view of culture is to use the Cultural Web (Johnson, Scholes and Whittington, 2008). The elements of the web, listed in Figure 4.1, provide a way of viewing the culture within the so-called *organizational paradigm*. The purpose of carrying out this exercise, which is sometimes known as a *cultural audit*, *cultural snapshot* or a *cultural analysis*, is to be able to describe what culture exists in the organization, and whether or not it influences your wellbeing strategy. Chances are, it most definitely will. However, it is important to focus on just what aspects you expect to cause conflicts with what you are trying to achieve. What are going to be the greatest areas of challenge for you to overcome? This can be enormously helpful in avoiding some of the problems and pitfalls that a wellbeing strategy might introduce.

Figure 4.1   Organizational paradigm components

SOURCE adapted from Johnson, Scholes and Whittington (2008)

Organizational paradigm

Let us look at these aspects in greater detail. We would like to point out here that there are, of course, other ways to look at culture, but this seems to work well for us, and has stood the test of time. The organizational paradigm is constructed using six areas for consideration, taken largely to represent the taken-for-granted assumptions of an organization. The paradigm, in this sense, was spoken about by Thomas Kuhn (2012), an American philosopher, who offered a view on how innovation occurred. He proposed that acceptable practices were conducted within the paradigm, what he called normal science. When something new came along it was tested until it became feasible to institute a paradigm shift, where a new working paradigm became the norm. This paradigm describes how an organization operates and runs on a day-to-day basis. As we aim to embed wellbeing within this paradigm, it is critical to have some idea of what else is going on. The 'what else' informally is the key – what workers do, say, how they behave, feel about work and so on. You will see that these also incorporate, in many ways, Schein's three levels of culture (2010), these being 1) artefacts, 2) espoused values and 3) assumptions and beliefs. What stands out here is that these may or may not be tangible, and are often abstract. For example, values are dominant within such working paradigms. What you will get a feel for is that you are looking, for some of these elements, at how people feel, perceive or react to a particular circumstance. Other elements, the so-called hard elements, relate to more scientific criteria. These may include structure charts, lines of management etc.

Stories

So, starting at the top, as depicted in Figure 4.1, we begin with stories. This is one of the so-called soft aspects and can be the lens that says it all. Requiring you to speak to people who experience the workplace, you need to establish what people talk about at work. This is not only internally, but may extend to complete outsiders who have nothing to do with the company. It may also be what people tell new entrants, contractors, part-time staff, customers, suppliers and so on. You may enquire if there are differences in the narrative, and why that might be thus. This is a good way to establish the history of the organization, the past, present and future. People often describe the heroes, villains and mavericks in the organization, and what behaviours they exhibit, what norms they may deviate from, strengths and weaknesses, and so on. Touching again on informality, there may be a number of conversations going on, which is interesting in itself and may illustrate the extent to which employees buy in to the values of the organization. If there appears to be incongruence, can the origin of this be readily identified? This is important to the wellbeing approach to be taken, if it is to be effective.

Symbols

Our next area is that of symbols, a further soft aspect. Some organizations are highly symbolic, and almost all have at least one logo and company communications format. What we are looking for here is how the organization rewards its people, how it portrays itself internally and externally, what aspects it promotes or demotes. In the workplace, how are staff rewarded for a good job, or extra effort in times of need, and are these rewards visible to others? For example, do workers get time off, extra perks or financial rewards? Do they get an e-mail from the boss, thanking them?

A further insightful way to look at symbols is in the office structure. Where do the executives sit? Are they accessible? Is there a strong chain of command, is there a formal address to senior people within the organization? Have people self-declared grand titles of office? What privileges do different layers enjoy within the organization? These privileges can be relatively minor, such as car-parking places, the biggest office, the latest tech etc. These points contribute enormously when trying to embed wellbeing. If you consider the notion of organizational fairness and wellbeing, the links can be made vividly through this lens. We acknowledge that some of the other areas are very often symbolic, but having a deeper understanding of the symbolic nature (or not) of an organization can provide great insight into those other elements.

Rituals and routines

The final soft aspect is that of rituals and routines. Closely linked to symbols these are used to clarify what routines are emphasized highly, and what are not so. Often expressed as 'the way we do things around here', this can often be the key to understanding informal and formal working practices, and very often the gulf that sits between. The informal working practices may have been in existence for many years, as in our case study above describing the UK parliament, so it is important that you not only understand what is going on, but also why. Getting this wrong can often lead to new initiatives going widely astray. One of the issues that organizations often debate is that of the efficacy of staff training programmes for a host of differing reasons. These can range from new equipment being bought in to changes in legislation requiring different approaches. Further examples of routines and rituals that are of significant challenge to most is that of recruitment, retention, promotion and exit policies. Most organizations seem to toy with the approach to these things on a regular basis, but negative culture can quietly undermine this process in the background. A further illustration that can provide a good example is who associates with who, and doing what, outside of working hours. Are there deep social groups? Are people married, or having relationships within the hierarchy? Does management support or dissuade this? You may expect to find this in family firms, of course, but in big public-service organizations this can often be seen as nepotistic and, as such, questions of organizational fairness may come in to play.

Power structures

We now move on to what are known as the hard aspects of this model. Hopefully you will now be able to begin, at least, to see how this can help in the design and implementation of your wellbeing strategy. The first aspect we describe is the power structure. This tells you a great deal about the organization, whether public or private sector, large or small, local or global. One of the main tenets of power structures is that those carrying most power nearly always dictate the mission, visions and values of an organization. It is wise to align with these as wellbeing is taken forward. To develop a wellbeing strategy at odds with the existing beliefs system may take you in an unfavourable direction. So, in terms of power it may be helpful to identify how power is distributed. Is there an informal and formal structure, are there power brokers, are there those who hold power for other reasons (eg partners of the executive)? Power is a fascinating concept in an organization, possibly because it is almost always not where you think! Organizations transiting through change are constantly challenged by blockages in the power or decision tree. It is important to have clarity on this.

Organizational structures

The second hard aspect is that of organizational structures. Here you are looking at how things are set up, reporting lines and so on. Are these flat and informal, or rigid and hierarchical? This can tell you a lot, especially if they do not accord with the rest of what is going on in the company. The cultural cues to look out for here are alignment, informality and, to some extent, the working assumptions (unwritten rules). These can be difficult to spot on occasion, especially for outsiders, and are often the pitfall of consultants. This is because the minute they leave, people revert back to the 'way things are done around here'. So, what we are saying is there are organizational structures in place, ie written processes, procedures, hierarchies and so on, but are these actually adhered to? If you are trying to launch a meaningful wellbeing programme in to the mix you will need a good understanding of this. For example, do the structures support collaboration or competition? What types of power do they support? We hope this is all starting to make a little more sense now, and will help you to understand how wellbeing fits.

Control systems

The final part of the cultural jigsaw, in these terms, is the mystery of control systems at play within an organization. We take particular note of these because they include elements such as reward and recognition systems within organizations, what the organization values in what employees do, how much interplay and competition there is within the organization, and so on. We also find here legislative requirements that organizations operate within, the management information systems, performance management approaches, the type of leadership style condoned, budget restraints and some political elements if the organization works within these. This is the final hard aspect and again can yield insightful information to inform your wellbeing plans.

To conclude this commentary on the organizational paradigm, some insight into the six elements discussed above can help you to avoid many of the common pitfalls encountered when launching a wellbeing strategy into an organization. If you consider each of these in turn and plan carefully you should avoid these pitfalls and your wellbeing strategy will be successful.

Change readiness

The next area we are going to consider is change readiness, and the preparedness of the organization to incorporate wellbeing into its make-up. One of the seminal pieces of business literature that may help inform this area is to be found in Balogun and Hope-Hailey's Change Kaleidoscope (2008). Following on from what we have seen in the Cultural Web, the idea posited is that most organizations, if not all, go through change programmes. Some public-sector employers find themselves in almost a constant change programme, as government demands of them are constantly changing and becoming increasingly demanding. The model suggests that organizations consider who is responsible for leading the proposed change and that they are suitable, whether a single person or a team. In terms of wellbeing, this may be an optimal way of implementing the programme. The notion of readiness should be, in part, half done. This is because the approach is predicated on that the need, identified by those employed, has already been recognized and accepted. Getting 'change or wellbeing' agents then deployed to champion the approach should follow on as part of this approach.

Taken with the Cultural Web, this approach can help you overcome some of the problems and pitfalls that the introduction of a wellbeing strategy can bring. Having expertise to help you over these early hurdles can be very helpful indeed. We have provided insight into the areas to be considered carefully here, and of course there may be many other considerations, dependent on the particular circumstances of the organization and the context it is operating within.

Stigma

Our final note in this chapter seeks to identify the damaging nature of stigma, especially around mental health. The 'Time to Change' movement in the UK has sought to end mental health discrimination, and has largely succeeded. The ambition of the movement is to make mental health discussions the norm, championing the proposition that people can talk openly about mental health problems. This has also received full support from the Royal Foundation, in the UK, and most notably the British royal family backing an openness about this previously taboo subject. This subject has been difficult for organizations, but we believe that the destigmatization of mental health, and encouraging open discussions in the workplace, is truly the right way to go. We would encourage inclusion of addressing or overcoming stigma in any wellbeing strategy and consider this an approach that all organizations should adopt. A vivid example is illustrated by Calnan (2017), reporting on a UK insurance company whereby 80 per cent of the managers considered that their staff would be comfortable discussing their mental health with them, when in fact 10 per cent of the employees felt the same. This is concerning when trying to create a working environment that inspires and promotes meaning and purpose.

Commentators on compassion in the workplace concur. Compassion is when people take the extra step from feeling sympathy or empathy and actually take measures to help improve the circumstances of another. We suggest that, in terms of stigma, this is the appropriate path to take. In relation to work, you may expect increasing levels of commitment, or buy-in, and thus from a business sense it is worthwhile. Of course, in our minds, the heart argument should always take precedence.

Summary

Like with any business strategy, wellbeing can have its problems if approached in a clumsy or ad hoc manner. The purpose of this chapter has been to draw your attention to some of the more common problems and pitfalls we have seen when trying to implement a workforce wellbeing approach, or strategy. Of course, not all of these issues will emerge, but it is important that you can spot what is going on. The main aim is to take your workforce with you on the journey – and understanding how they may perceive your intentions is critical. Not only can this be costly, and potentially embarrassing, but it also threatens the psychological contract an employee can have with their employers. In other words, you can unintentionally make things worse, with mixed messages or confusing engagement. Like with other elements of work strategy, it is important that the plan is coherent and meaningful, is positive in tone, and the workforce can identify with it easily. With this in mind, the importance of promoting a growth mindset approach is key, allowing learning to be made from errs, not seeking to blame or criticize. These things will make a huge difference.

This chapter has also examined some common errs when organizations implement wellbeing using management by metrics or championing sporting metaphor. To help you work through this we have also included some details of cultural tools that can help you make sense of what is going on, and how to ensure as far as possible that the strategy works. Like with surveying, it is the attitudes and perceptions of your workforce that you are looking to influence, reality may not be the issue. The use of the Cultural Web is an excellent way to consider the requirements within an organization, and what may be the sensitive areas to be considered. This also helps you to think about best fit, what to put in place first, and who may be on board. Change management, and we will return to this later in the book, is a big source of stress for any workforce. However, it is necessary in nearly all organizations, especially with the demands of the marketplace and the impact of ever-complex technology. We have offered some advice on how to approach this within your plans also. Stigma around mental health problems is often corrosive and can impact hugely on the working climate, this is as important as other aspects we have spoken about in this chapter and should also be a deliberation in your strategy.

Key takeaways from this chapter

Focus

Keeping your wellbeing strategy on track is really important. As things develop it is easy to get side-tracked, new ideas emerge and there are always lots of shiny new things to shift your attention.

Mindset

Keep a growth mindset – accept things are often uncertain and it is a complex world out there. Use mistakes as opportunities to learn. Try not to look to blame people if things go astray. People don't often make mistakes on purpose and, as the saying goes, those who have never made a mistake have never made anything.

Management by metrics

We do not subscribe to the mantra that if you can measure it you can manage it. This type of approach is a real source of stress, and you will find people hitting the target but missing the point. The target culture of the 1990s was quite damaging in terms of wellbeing, and rarely people like being managed by numbers.

Sporting analogy

There are a number of areas where these are not helpful to businesses. If you are training to be the best you can be at a point in time in the future when you are competing, this is fair enough. For others in their day-to-day working routines goal setting can have positive outcomes, but they have to be realistic and sustainable.

Flow

We subscribe to being in the moment, when time stands still. Having meaning and purpose in your life, being in a state of flow, is what we consider to be the crux of wellbeing.

Culture

No good business book is without some commentary on culture. In terms of wellbeing it is a big actor, perhaps the biggest. Making sure your organization's culture aligns to your wellbeing strategy is critical. We provide an excellent model to help you work through your own organizational paradigm. This will help you situate your wellbeing approach within the context of your own working environment.

Change readiness

Change can be the biggest stressor in the workplace, but unfortunately is the reality for most organizations. Preparing for change and being aware of the impact it can have on your people is key.

Stigma

A final word in this chapter goes to the subject of stigma and mental health. This is often very damaging for individuals, and we suggest you foster a culture where not only is it acceptable, but actually people are encouraged to discuss mental health issues openly. This environment will help create, as we previously discussed, a culture of acceptance and understanding. People are not at their best all the time, and you should accept this. Kindness and compassion towards employees who, for whatever reason, are struggling, will be repaid over and over again.

References

Balogun, J and Hope-Hailey, V (2008) *Exploring Strategic Change*, 3rd edn, Prentice Hall, Harlow

Calnan, M (2017) [accessed 4 August 2018] One In Four Employees With Mental Health Issues Say Work is the Cause, *People Management*, 28 March [Online] http://www2.cipd.co.uk/pm/peoplemanagement/b/weblog/ archive/2017/03/28/one-in-four-employees-with-mental-health-issues-say-work-is-the-cause.aspx

Collingridge, J, Shipman, T and Pogrund, G (2017) [accessed 4 August 2018] Labour Hushes Up Second 'Suicide' After Sex Claims, *The Times* [Online] https://www.thetimes.co.uk/article/labour-hushes-up-second-suicide-after-sex-claims-zz950mwgt

Csikszentmihalyi, M (1992) *Flow: The psychology of happiness*, Rider, London

Dweck, C S (2006) *Mindset: The new psychology of success*, 1st edn, Random House, New York

Guilfoyle, S (2013) *Intelligent Policing: How systems thinking methods eclipse conventional management practice*, Triarchy Press, Devon

Hood, C (1991) A public management for all seasons?, *Public Administration*, **69** (1), pp 3–19

Johnson, G, Scholes, K and Whittington, R (2008) *Exploring Corporate Strategy*, 8th edn, Pearson Education, London

Kuhn, T S (2012) *The Structure of Scientific Revolutions*, 4th edn, University of Chicago Press, Chicago and London

Schein, E H (2010) *Organizational Culture and Leadership*, 4th edn, Jossey-Bass, San Francisco

Seligman, M (2011) *Flourish: A new understanding of happiness and well-being – and how to achieve them*, Nicholas Brealey, London

Syed, M (2015) *Black Box Thinking: Why most people never learn from their mistakes – but some do*, John Murray, London

Wright, O (2017) [accessed 4 August 2018] Theresa May calls for new 'culture of respect' amid Westminster sleaze scandal, *The Times* [Online] https://www.thetimes.co.uk/article/theresa-may-calls-for-new-culture-of-respect-amid-westminster-sleaze-scandal-6qv6x5fm9

Monitoring and evaluating 05

Introduction

Revisiting a number of key constructs, this chapter aims to suggest how wellbeing initiatives can be monitored and evaluated, reviewing examples from practice and placing them in the context of valid and robust research to strengthen their appeal. We provide professional advice on what to look out for, how frequently to evaluate, and the importance of these processes in systematically reviewing your people strategy.

Being open to challenge can be difficult, but we argue that workplace environments that permit periodic review will benefit enormously in terms of staff engagement and wellbeing. We start by looking at the key advantages of strategy setting, and what this can do for your organization. Taking a journey through the key elements, we discuss the strategic importance of goal setting in any business, and how that links in with your mission, vision and values.

Constructing a strategy is important, and it must cohere. That is to say, that it enables the right hand of your business to effectively communicate and interact with the left; something that is not always apparent.

We then move on to the all-important measurement of wellbeing, what that looks like and how it can inform any interventions or business changes you may consider making. Of course, these may originate from what you have garnered while doing these exercises. We have already discussed the pitfalls that measurement can bring, so this is more of a good practice example, written in a positive frame.

This chapter then explores effectiveness and efficiency. After all, that is the aim of all this collectively. This will also illustrate the key role that wellbeing plays in these areas of business. We then look at performance and productivity, linking academic research that will hopefully convince you that the outcomes of a well-considered and executed wellbeing strategy will pay dividends, making your organization a better place to be.

The focus then moves on to ethics, one of the cornerstones, and origins, of meaning and purpose in working life. The chapter concludes with a discussion about evaluation. This is all-important – knowing that you are going along the right lines, creating your own evidence of success, and making meaningful changes for the benefit of your workforce based on what you have learnt. This growth mindset is where you should aspire to be. Having a learning culture, not seeking blame, but business improvement, should be the aim. We suggest this will impact on all the aforementioned, and firmly place your organization in a great place; a place where people want to work and where you accommodate meaning, purpose, happiness and prosperity.

Strategy

We have already stated the criticality of ensuring that your wellbeing strategy sits firmly within an organization's general working premise. We have recommended that fact-finding exercises are conducted to ensure the strategy adds meaning and purpose within your organization, these being the key tenets of wellbeing. Furthermore, the majority of research suggests this is optimum in terms of outcome. The engagement with and dissemination to your workforce is equally as important, to reiterate key text on this: 'Deciding strategy is only one step; strategic decisions need to be communicated' (Johnson, Scholes and Whittington, 2008: 574). Furthermore, 'middle managers in particular are likely to be key since they are often tasked with making senior management plans' (Balogun, 2007: 81).

We also consider the importance of annual strategy reviews as it is good practice to look at wellbeing periodically in terms of best fit. Change in organizations is very often the status quo. What we are suggesting is that if there are big changes in size, policy, procedure, management changes and so on, a recap and communication of the wellbeing strategy should also be included as best practice. To quote the great Henry Mintzberg, 'Companies must remake themselves into places of engagement, where people are committed to one another and their enterprise' (2009: 140). Not forgetting, 'for every new strategy, there should be a communications strategy to match' (Johnson, Scholes and Whittington, 2008: 574). We will discuss performance later in this chapter, but productivity and performance are some of the key outcomes for an effective wellbeing approach.

Goals

It is most likely no surprise that any organization needs a set of goals, and in terms of wellbeing this should be no different. What is probably not as apparent is how these fit in with the overall strategic direction; where you want to get to, so to speak. We will discuss mission and vision shortly, but first the actionable goals. Goals must be, at some point at least, achievable. Setting outlandish or entirely aspirational goals is not particularly useful when set in the context of wellbeing. For example, goals such as eradicating all ill health and suchlike are unlikely ever to be realized, and employees soon become alert to this and thus they are not valued or aspired to. There is also the point of mixing up goals with the mission and values and, though often confusing, they are – or should be – different things. So, the goals when laying out your wellbeing plans should be set around making life at work as good as it can be, or not doing things that would compromise an employee's health and wellbeing. We acknowledge that in some countries health and safety legislates for this. Also, be careful not to have too many goals in relation to wellbeing. You want to avoid this being a list, if at all possible.

Under the goals, which should be a simple statement, there ought to be objectives outlining specifically how you intend to achieve this. The goals and objectives, as well as being achievable, should also be measurable. That is, how do you know when you have achieved them? What does success look like? With the end in mind, this should steer you in decision making about your goal setting. It is also important to keep in mind why you are actually doing whatever it is. Will these 'things' help the organization in some way? As well as the company being profitable, does it maintain responsibility for what it does (often referred to as corporate social responsibility)? The bottom line is that you should take care in defining your goals, and ensure they are both actionable and achievable.

Monitoring the goals is relatively straightforward. The objectives set to deliver the goals should be drafted with enough detail to allow for the checking of progress against them. In the same manner, the evaluation of goals should be relatively simple. Asking questions such as to what extent have they been achieved, or are on track? Having such structures in place is not only good business management, but it also allows for detailed progress reporting when required. This makes life easy (less stressful) for all, and ought to be adopted as best practice.

Vision

An organization's vision can be slightly more creative when it comes to wellbeing: phrases like world class and industry leading may spring to mind. This statement describes, in essence, where the organization sees its own future. What it will be, what it will be seen as by others. The vision statement may include aspirational references, or the road map, as some refer to it. As we referred to in goals, a vision statement is a relatively short sentence, typically about 3–30 words long. A further point to be made is that a vision normally stays in place for a number of years, unlike goals, which can be refreshed more periodically. This usually coincides with the mid-to long-term strategy, and helps to articulate as such. It could also work in developing a strategic focus, which again sets out a few aspirational headlines. As such, the vision should articulate more than just a catchy slogan for the organization's posters and website. It should be considered and authentic.

A wellbeing strategy has the aim of improving the physical, psychological and social health of employees, so a vision statement could be carved out of this, in terms of the wellbeing strategy. So, maybe it may outline what the direction is internally, via management styles, what this means for users, or customers of the organization, and what that means for the profitability or sustainability of the organization.

Mission

A mission statement normally involves some sort of narrative to detail how you might achieve your goals, including the aspirations of the vision to achieve this through aligning people with the purpose of the business. Although these all seem like flowery terms, the structures are actually useful in constructing both the strategy that people work for and the narrative ordering of how to describe what it is you are actually doing, and where you are trying to get to. This is very important in terms of clarity, mission clarity if you wish, and also engagement with your workforce. When we look at what a workforce values in terms of its leaders, a clear sense of direction is often prioritized. This should align with strategic capabilities, so is not too aspirational and can be realistically achieved by the workforce.

Values

When we consider values, these can be split into personal and organizational, with definitions including the notion that values are the key to effective wellbeing, providing a framework for ethics or the principles by which we work. We say notion because values do not really lend themselves to being a descriptive list, but something more personally intrinsic. Shalom Schwartz, creator of the theory of basic human values, described personal values as, 'concepts or beliefs that relate to desirable end-states or behaviours, transcend specific situations, guide selection or evaluation of behaviour and events, and are ordered by relative importance' (1996: 4).

An important point here is that when looking at values we are not really talking about the monetary worth but more the psychological boundaries within which we work. These include looking at what we hold dear, what is important to the organization, and so on. The purpose of an organization can be strengthened by strong values and these should be articulated and embedded, allowing employees to take meaning and purpose from their working life that is congruent with the values they hold. This can often be a tricky dilemma, as you may find this conflicting with making profit or leading in a competitive market. How far will you have to go to succeed, and will this breach the values you may wish to work within?

When values are compromised, workers will often feel like they are also being compromised. So, how do these acceptable standards of behaviour work into your wellbeing strategy? We strongly recommend that this is a consultative process, and the proposed values are set in conjunction with the workforce. Exercises such as world café conversations or focus groups can be used to explore and discuss organizational and individual values and alignment. The buy-in is essential, as with all strategic decisions.

There are interesting comparisons with corporate social responsibility and how this impacts on a workforce. This is beyond the scope of what we are suggesting here but nevertheless is a fascinating area of work. When organizations take seriously the values they hold, and that of their workforce, the working environment can be improved markedly.

The relationship between values, behaviours and culture, which we have discussed elsewhere in this book, are inextricably linked. The Engage for Success work noted, 'Engaged organizations have strong and authentic values, with clear evidence of trust and fairness based on mutual respect, where two-way promises and commitments, between employers and staff, are understood and fulfilled' (MacLeod and Clarke, 2009). A further related topic is that of ethics, which we discuss below.

Ethics

Closely associated with values are ethics. In fact, most combine the two in strategic documents. Ethics is a branch of moral philosophy, closely associated with doing the right things for the right reasons. It derives from the Greek word *ethikos*, from ethos, which means habit or custom. It has also been interpreted as a system of moral principles that govern a person's behaviour or activity. It can be divided into three areas: metaethics, normative ethics and applied ethics. These describe various levels of living a good and moral life, one that has rights and responsibilities at heart. These involve ethical dilemmas, ethical decision making, amongst other things. Metaethics deal with the history and the origins of ethical principles and moral judgement. What is right and wrong, and dilemmas are dealt with in the area of normative ethics, and we see a lot of organizational training programmes using dilemmas to tease out the basic points of ethics. These form the basis of asking groups of employees to consider various workplace scenarios, perhaps where there is no right or wrong answer, and to debate what the various options are through the lens of ethics. Issues such as bending the rules, or making exceptions for individuals, often form the foundation for such exercises. The main consideration is that, strictly speaking, there is no right or wrong answer, it is the human interaction, and the impact on others that steers the conclusion. Finally, applied ethics takes a look at the big issues, such as the ethics (controversy) of intervening in Iraq, Afghanistan or Syria perhaps.

The bottom line with ethics is that, in terms of the relationship with wellbeing, it is inseparable. Meaning and purpose in life are closely linked to moral philosophy, the 'why' as Simon Sinek refers to it. The ethical rules that apply to considering right or wrong almost always cohere with what we consider to be morally good for us or what makes us feel happy, subjectively well – although, on the whole, ethics is usually about the impact on others rather than self-interest. Nevertheless, ethics align as the greater good.

Measurement

There are a number of views on measurement. These are largely in respect of the behaviours that they often drive to achieve a goal. That said, managing wellbeing needs to include measurements, and here we will discuss sensible approaches that can be taken. Generally speaking there are two types of measurement – quantitative and qualitative. Arguments abound as to which is the most effective, including a mixed methods approach. For simplification's sake we can say that quantitative methods involve numbers, percentages and so on to establish pictures of the landscape, and qualitative involves a descriptive picture, through stories or accounts, for example.

However, very thick text books have been written on the pros and cons, whys and wherefores of these methods, and combinations thereof, and you will soon see that this is a complex area of business, or even a business in itself. If we consider that managing wellbeing could be considered a risk management process, this may assist in looking at proactivity, interventions and indeed different methods to analyse direction and progress. So, identify the areas of wellbeing you intend to focus on, analyse what is known and evaluate or prioritize, look at what you are going to do (the treatment) and your strategy to monitor and review. Overall, ask yourself what benefits is the strategy providing to your employees, and your customers? How are you better off by having this?

To provide further detail, if we consider what we need to measure we can look at what we are going to be doing, what are the risks, what are the benefits, and how we 'quantify' these. Once this has been done we now need to decide what our mechanism will be for monitoring these facets. Again, we look to how we 'quantify' these. Using instruments such as the stress assessment tool – ASSET – can assist in providing clarity. These break down employees' attitudes and perceptions on a number of wellbeing issues. Information can also be gleaned via focus groups, interviews with employees, keeping diaries or logs and, of course, traditional sickness data.

One of the issues for organizations is around the length of time between measurements, or if there is a case for constant measurement. This is not straightforward, and we consider this down to the requirements of the organization, though it seems sensible that if there are identified issues, these measurements can be useful to ensure the right approaches are being taken. There are arguments for a continual cycle, and also for incorporating this into routine management practices.

One of the issues with measurement, or assessment of any kind in fact, is that they can cause unintended consequences. These may include resentment, suspicion or issues of trust in employees. They may question why you need to measure – is it that they do not believe what is being said, or what behaviours are manifesting as a result of the measurement? For example, is the treatment changing behaviours, or the fact they are being measured? See, for example, the

Hawthorne Experiments (Mayo, 1946). The way to respond here is to be open, honest, transparent and proactive in the engagement of the workforce. As the saying goes, 'trust arrives on foot and leaves on horseback'. That is, it may take years to build trust in your workforce, but literally seconds to destroy it. One way to destroy it is to be clumsy with measuring any kind of performance or productivity metric. Therefore, there needs to be an overemphasis that this is required to improve working practice, ensure things in the workplace are improving, and to show a genuine commitment to the workforce. As with other feelings we have mentioned, trust is difficult to quantify (but you will know when you've lost it!) and can be difficult to earn. Therefore, a notion of success can be introduced that is gauged through measurement. This framing helps employees to understand and invest in the purpose of metrics in order to allow them to flourish in the workforce, in whatever way they consider that to be.

Other measures that are popular in terms of wellbeing address a host of areas. For measuring personal resilience, you may employ the six-item Brief Resiliency Scale (Smith *et al*, 2008). To measure perceived organizational support, you may use a scale developed by Eisenberger *et al* (1986), which seeks to establish to what extent employees trust that their employer cares about them. The theory being that if they do, the employees are more likely to be more productive and loyal, and as a result a strong psychological contract exists and performance improves. This particular scale, as they are referred to, has 16 items (questions) and probes issues that highlight value at work.

The International Physical Activity Questionnaire (Craig *et al*, 2003) uses 27 questions to ascertain a population's physical activity levels. It is a popular measure when considering mobilizing an otherwise sedentary workforce, where perhaps the workforce is largely office based and the majority of work is performed sitting at a desk. These question sets can be a prompt for action, engaging with employees and nudging them to think about their physical activity, lifestyle, and how that impacts on their work and private life. This can also have the impact of perceived organizational support (as mentioned in the previous survey), as it brings to the fore notions that the organization cares for their physical, as well as emotional, wellbeing.

We have already mentioned our next survey instrument – ASSET – and it is one we have employed on many occasions to test many different occupations. These organizations were from both the public sector and the private sector and included manufacturing plants, local education authorities, large county councils, police forces, universities, the prison service, and various other service providers. ASSET, which stands for A Shortened Stress Evaluation Tool (Faragher, Cooper and Cartwright, 2004), is a further diagnostic that surveys the workforce and examines the extent to which individuals and groups are affected by stress, identifying at-risk areas and providing a normative data set by which to compare sectors, individuals or groups of people against each other. ASSET uses six areas, referred to as six essentials to probe perceptions about work relationships, work–life balance, workload overload, job security, control, and resources and communications. A further attitudinal question set probes perceived commitment of organization to employees, and perceived commitment of employees to the organization.

We ourselves have used this survey instrument to look at stress in policing, both in the UK and the United States. What this approach effectively does is give you evidence to make the case for interventions, to test interventions, and to evaluate the interventions longitudinally (see for example Hesketh, Cooper and Ivy, 2017). The information that emerges from these surveys is vital to inform good decision making, and to look at improved ways of future working. These take into account organizational, team and individual experiences that can help improve wellbeing strategy. For example, we used ASSET to research the efficacy of resilience training among UK police (Hesketh, Cooper and Ivy, 2018). This subsequently went on to inform national strategy and highlight the criticality of personal resilience within police officers and staff.

In Table 5.1 we have outlined some of the question sets that you may find useful and which have already been validated through their established use in the field of organizational wellbeing and associated topics (of which there are many). That is, you can rely on them to give you valid and reliable results. A final word of caution on this is that surveying properly is a highly skilled profession, with many pitfalls in its own right. We suggest you access professional advice

Table 5.1 Example of wellbeing question sets

Area measured	Name	No of questions
1 Six essentials	ASSET	36
2 Resiliency	Brief Resiliency Scale	6
3 Personal resilience	Connor-Davidson Resilience Scale	25
4 Hardiness	Dispositional Resilience Scale	12
5 Stress	Stress Mindset Questionnaire general	8
6 Resilience	Adverse Childhood Experiences Scale	5
7 Coping	Cope Inventory	13
8 Burnout	Copenhagen Burnout Inventory	7
9 Empathy	Empathy Quotient (short version)	8
10 Presenteeism	Stress-Related Presenteeism Scale	6
11 Life satisfaction	Office of National Statistics	1
12 Happiness	Office of National Statistics	1
13 Anxiety	Office of National Statistics	1
14 Eudaemonia	Office of National Statistics	1
15 Stress	Police Stress Questionnaire and Organizational	PSQ-Op = 20 PSQ-Org = 20
16 Physical activity	International Physical Activity Questionnaire	27
17 Mental health	Psychological subscales	16
18 Trauma	Davidson Trauma Scale	17
19 Wellbeing	Wellbeing Process Questionnaire	33
20 Engagement	Utrecht Work Engagement Questionnaire	9
21 Lifestyle	Fast Alcohol Screening Test Tobacco Use Questionnaire	FAST = 4 TUQ = 9
22 Value at work	Scale of Perceived Organizational Support	16
23 Exercise motivation	Treatment Self-Regulation Questionnaire Perceived Competency Scale	15 4
24 Workability	Work Ability Index	1
25 Personality	Eysenck Personality Questionnaire	60

before embarking on surveying your workforce. This is both to ensure it is done properly and so that you can rely on the results that emerge. This is critical to any subsequent interventions and evaluation you do to remedy issues raised. You may receive many offers of help to formulate surveys and establish baseline information. We suggest, for this piece of work that will be pivotal to all that follows, it is always far better to set out on the right foot. Therefore, getting expert guidance is strongly advised.

Data

This is, or can be, a minefield. With new rules and regulations regularly coming into being, largely reacting to new technologies, this is rarely simple. Two aspects impact: first, is what you want to establish. Second, is if you can legally and ethically capture, store and utilize personal data for these purposes. This needs some serious thought. What you want to avoid is setting up data capture, either a one-off survey, or more periodically automatically captured metrics, to later find out that the practice is illegal or unethical. Both will have a damaging effect on your workforce and organization, both short and long term. There are two types of data, primary and secondary. Primary data is what you capture for a particular purpose, by whatever means. Secondary is when you utilize existing data, for whatever reason. These can be existing work records, right through to online data samples (eg Office of National Statistics). It is important to consider what the data is going to be used for, whatever the source.

The recent changes in (EU) legislation covering all sorts of privacy issues, and largely to combat considerable data intrusions for the purpose of marketing and identity theft, have turned this world into a wasp's nest. The General Data Protection Regulation (GDPR) is a new EU law that came into effect on 25 May 2018 to replace the previous Data Protection Act. It is the biggest overhaul of data protection legislation for over 25 years and introduced new requirements for how organizations process personal data. It is worth spending some time looking at the main concepts of this to map progress that involves some element of collecting and tracking the progress of employers.

There are many websites dedicated to explaining in further detail, and a web search will quickly establish these. In the final chapter of this book we outline the concepts of the GDPR, legislatively, that you need to be concerned with as these may focus your approach.

Effectiveness

Here we discuss effectiveness in terms of wellbeing and wellbeing interventions in organizations. These, occasionally, cannot be easy to establish with any degree of ease, especially in the early days, as often people will question differing approaches to wellbeing. In fact, wellbeing is not a universally accepted set of propositions, it is far more complex than that. As such, creating any sort of gauge of effectiveness can be difficult. However, it is worth persevering with, as the results can be transformational. When people seek work, they are often focused on how the proposed job fits them. They are motivated in a number of ways: money, satisfaction, sense of community service, job fulfilment and so on. People may take on work for any of the above reasons, but if the job does not deliver they may soon start to look elsewhere for a better deal. This may not result in them leaving, by the way, but may result in them withdrawing discretionary effort – the effort they give above and beyond what is asked for, or paid for. This effort is very often the big difference in the organization's bottom line.

Organizational effectiveness seeks ways to ensure, through workforce satisfaction rather than punitive actions, that organizations can take advantage of great working environments where the workforce draw meaning and purpose and therefore willingly give more of themselves towards the organizational aims. Effectiveness should also cohere with the objectives, as Ackoff (1999) observes – effectiveness is evaluated efficiency, which leads very nicely on to our next area.

Efficiency

Although often used together with effectiveness, efficiency has some subtle differences to effectiveness. Efficiency relates to using resources that are available as effectively as is feasible. This is sometimes viewed through a lens of waste, in terms of both processes as well as materials. What activity do you do that adds no value to your business or its workforce? In terms of wellbeing, employees can be demotivated by work that is bureaucratic or viewed as unnecessary, and therefore a focus on efficiency can be a useful component to measure. Efficiency has the scope to be measured and used within your wellbeing strategy to gauge how much effort, money or other processes are being used in a useful and productive way. For example, organizations may subscribe to medical services, such as employee assistance programmes. What an efficiency measure would help you do is to gauge how many are using the service and if the service is utilized reasonably for the amount you are paying for it. Effectiveness would allow you to assess if the service is worth having, efficiency helps you quantify the use, value for money and to strategically plan.

Productivity

This and the next area – performance – are where the benefits of having really good workplace wellbeing approaches really comes into action. Productivity and performance are always improved when you have an effective wellbeing strategy in place. If you are in the business of manufacturing or selling something, this is usually quite easy to see. If you are in the services sector you may see this through other lenses. In the UK, productivity is one of the issues challenging most companies. The obvious downside to poor productivity is that profits suffer, but also employees themselves suffer, with living standards and quality of life issues also beginning to emerge. We know that people who are healthy, happy and connected at work are more productive. Research from Robertson Cooper found that people with low wellbeing estimated that they were only productive 67 per cent of the time, while those who had high wellbeing were productive at work 87 per cent of the time (2017). In terms of monitoring and evaluation, it is probably better to consider how you are going to establish a means of measuring productivity, bearing in mind all we have spoken about regarding pitfalls. After all, you do not want to inadvertently reduce productivity by using clumsy measures.

Performance

The general aim of this book describes what we ascribe to performance. That is, the improvement of employee engagement; decrease in staff turnover; reduced sickness absenteeism, presenteeism and leaveism; and a more dedicated and happy workforce. When this is achieved through what is often termed 'business as usual' it is undoubtedly indicative of great performance. The workforce will experience meaning and purpose, feel supported and feel their working life is worthwhile. This is no easy feat and being able to describe when you have reached this status quo may be even more difficult. Many assign metrics as to what good performance may look like, how many, how often, how much waste, and so on. Measuring people performance can be quite tricky though. What we have described here are elements of emotional buy-in. Akin to relationships, these may ebb and flow. It is unlikely you will be able to sustain 'first day in the job' performance from all employees. But, skilfully crafted, you may get close, and certainly become more efficient.

Happiness

In essence, this is the very point of this book. We subscribe to a happy workforce as delivering on all of the above elements, and here we are not referring to the Prozac leadership descriptors offered by Collinson (2012), where one has positivity beyond the norm. In fact, happiness can involve times of discomfort, the highs and the lows. It seems the key here is that happy people do not disguise negative emotions, they are open and honest, they meet setbacks head on, acknowledge them and push through. This appears congruent with theories around post-traumatic growth – what doesn't kill you makes you stronger, as they say.

What we are talking about here of course is subjective wellbeing, so wonderfully described by Sonja Lyubomirsky (2013) in her book, *The How of Happiness*. In this she discusses whether it is possible to become happier, the impact of traumatic events and how to be sustainably happy, drawing on some of the work we have already discussed in this book.

For business, happiness is good, and happiness is good for business! However, there is a lot of literature discussing the relationship between wealth and happiness, love and happiness, and inner prosperity and financial wealth. Congruent with research suggesting that the struggle is part of the journey, most wealth-happiness research concludes with the summary 'up to a point'. We would argue that, like good leadership, inner happiness is brought about by personal outlook, commitment, social interaction and caring, and challenge to achieve goals. In a study of more than 10,000 participants from 48 countries, psychologists Ed Diener, Richard Lucas and Shigehiro Oishi discovered that people from around the world rated happiness as being more important than other highly desirable personal outcomes, such as having meaning in life, becoming rich and getting into heaven (2007). However, a greater sense of meaning in life was found in poorer populations. Happiness has also been linked to better health, improved immunity from disease and higher creativity.

When it comes to measuring and monitoring happiness there are a number of approaches. One sort of knows when the workforce is happy, but rarely is this 'feeling' sufficient enough to get to grips with the social sciences favourite as 'to what extent?' Fortunately, there are a number of tools to help. Subjective wellbeing, or happiness, has a number of validated questionnaires that you can use to measure just how happy your workforce is. As well as the ONS scale mentioned in Table 5.1 there are other specific happiness scales. Lyubomirsky (mentioned above) and Lepper developed the Subjective Happiness Scale (1999); Diener *et al* (1985) introduced the Satisfaction with Life Scale; there is the Oxford Happiness Inventory (Hills and Argyle, 2002) and the Panas Scale (Watson, Clark and Tellegen, 1988).

Evaluation

One of the key success measures of any wellbeing strategy is gleaned from evaluation. As such, the evaluation needs to be robust and reliable. Arguably it may be a waste of time unless this is so. You may consider the validity of the evaluation dependent on it being carried out independently. However, if done in earnest, an internal evaluation is quite acceptable. We do see organizations forming peer support groups to effectively help each other through evaluation or audit. This can be good practice and worth considering.

So, what should an evaluation contain? For a start you need to know the starting point. This is also important when setting work in motion. Benchmarking the off position is very important and will help you track any improvements. This element involves capturing how people see their work, what the barriers are and what access to resources they have. You can also capture existing data that is held on systems, such as sickness levels, insubordination reports and numerous other metrics that help inform practice. If you measure performance or productivity in any fashion, these should also be captured to assess progress from the start.

As you set your strategy in motion, or any interventions or new ways of working, you should have some prior idea of how you are going to use numerous sources of information to evaluate the efficacy of your approach. We have already spoken in depth about staff surveys, which can be a great way of carrying out evaluation and gap analysis, and in Table 5.1 we have provided some examples of what may be contained in these. You may also look at any funding you may have received to carry out your plans, and any requirements for evaluation specified by these. Very often funding requires before-and-after evaluation by way of audit. This is done to ensure effective spend. You may also view this by how many staff hours are going to be involved in any project delivery, or strategy delivery.

The first steps may be to decide, probably at an executive level, what exactly a good outcome would look like. Then to establish what the inputs, measures and outputs will look like, and describe and document these. You may wish to keep in mind the earlier-mentioned rules most will operate under in respect of data protection also. The key things you need to ask are, does this approach improve the wellbeing of employees? Does what we are doing reduce sickness and improve productivity? We would suggest that you remain open to the idea that things may change and new things may become effective as your general workforce wellbeing improves. As the various interventions you may want to introduce permeate through your workforce you may want to assess where they have been most effective. Good evaluation can allow you to do this skilfully and with optimum results. Setting outcome measures is a good way to achieve this, for example what you may consider a good outcome is, and then how to look at indicators that will let you know when this seems to be coming into effect. The evaluation is key to this, but you have to set out with this in mind.

Summary

This chapter has been concerned with how wellbeing initiatives can be monitored and evaluated and, where appropriate, we have provided working examples from practice. Combining academic robustness with practice-based pragmatism illustrates the value of monitoring and evaluating. Learning how others have implemented wellbeing successfully can provide confidence in your own approach and is a great resource. As well as those discussed here there are thousands of online examples you can draw upon. We strongly suggest you do just that, using this book as a place to get started, to create a framework, and for reference as you progress. In this chapter we have called upon our own significant experiences, both academically and in practice, to provide professional advice on what to look out for. We have described the what, and how frequently, you should evaluate what you are doing and the importance of these processes in periodically reviewing your wellbeing, or people, strategy. Although on first glance this chapter may look like a glossary of terms, these concepts all form vital components to the success of any organizational wellbeing strategy.

Being open to challenge can be difficult, but we argue that workplace environments that are open to listening to their workforce and that permit periodic review, and optimally an independent review, will benefit enormously in terms of staff engagement and wellbeing. We began by looking at the key advantages of strategy setting, and what this can do for your organization. Taking a journey through the key elements we have discussed the strategic importance of goal setting. We claim that this is the same for any business. There are the important aspects of how that links in with your mission, vision and values; how it all aligns and coheres. It ought to be obvious if this is not the case, and we suggest this is carried out at an executive level ultimately, to ensure root and branch take-up. That is to say, that it enables the right hand of your business to effectively communicate and interact with the left – something we have found that in our many years of experience in this field is not always apparent.

This chapter then focuses your attention on the all-important measurement of wellbeing – what that looks like and how it can inform any innovations, interventions or business changes you may consider making. Of course, these may originate from what you have garnered doing these exercises. We have already discussed the pitfalls that measurement can bring, so this is more of a good-practice example, written in a positive frame with some measurement instruments, such as ASSET, that have worked effectively in many organizations as the key measurement approach.

This chapter has explored the subjects of effectiveness and efficiency. After all, that is the aim of all this wellbeing focus collectively. This has also illustrated the key role that wellbeing plays on all your areas of business. We then aligned performance and productivity, linking academic research that will have hopefully convinced you that the outcomes of a well-considered and executed wellbeing strategy will pay dividends.

Ethical considerations are one of the cornerstones, and origins, of meaning and purpose in working life, and in the course of this chapter we have outlined the main components and how they may be viewed, providing examples of exercises that can be carried out with your own workforce. The chapter concludes with a discussion about evaluation. This is all-important – knowing that you are traversing the right lines, creating your own evidence of success, and making meaningful changes for the benefit of your workforce based on what you have learnt. Having this growth mindset is where you should aspire to be, along with a learning culture, not seeking blame, but business improvement, should be the aim. This chapter should equip you with the key components of a wellbeing strategy; along with an operational delivery plan, it will provide you with a road map of what needs to be done, in what order, by who, and why. This should place your business as one where people want to work, and where you accommodate meaning, purpose, happiness and prosperity. This is brought about by placing your people firmly front and centre of all you do.

Machines and processes, whatever function they perform, will never reach the complexity of the human, with all their strengths, vulnerabilities and frailties. To get that right, or as right as possible, will place you firmly in front. The world of work is growing more complex by the day, with an overwhelming amount of new information being exposed to our workforce. Good wellbeing, considerately thought out and aimed at humanity must surely pay dividends for any organization. We acknowledge it is difficult, but this chapter should give you the information to make some considerable inroads into that complex world.

Key takeaways from this chapter

Strategy setting

Make sure that your wellbeing strategy fits in with what your business does, that it coheres with the main objectives. If this is the case you will have far more chance of implementing an effective strategy in terms of the wellbeing of your workforce. Also, there is far more chance of your workforce adhering to, and valuing, your approach to wellbeing. Look what you can strategically measure and evaluate over time and consider if this coheres with the rest of your organizational goals.

Goals

Set out clear and achievable goals. This is key to goal setting, for if they are too ambitious, or overstretch your workforce, they are unlikely to be aspired to, achieved or valued. Look at how you will monitor if your goals have been reached, or surpassed, and what that may look like.

Vision

In the dream, this is where your organization sees itself operating. This can be aspirational and usually consists only of a few words, or a strap line. In terms of wellbeing, this should correspond with the vision and have some recognition of the workforce position. You need to consider how you communicate your vision, and how you know that this has become a shared vision within your workforce. How will you monitor and measure the extent to which you have succeeded?

Mission

A mission statement may be slightly more descriptive and highlights the key tenets the organization may wish to pursue to achieve the vision. Once more, wellbeing inclusion is likely to have the overall effect of bringing the workforce on board and in pursuit of the aims of the business. As with the vision, is your workforce united behind the organizational mission? Are all employees putting a man on the moon?

Values

The values must align with the above, as when they are compromised the workforce may disengage. Here you can start to see how this maps the journey, through the lens of strategic direction down to the mechanics of how you get there, with wellbeing rooted firmly in the plans.

Ethics

A branch of moral philosophy and a lens through which to view right and wrong, the workforce can benefit from strong ethics. We discuss ethical dilemmas as a way of discussing issues that may often be seen as grey areas. Corporate social responsibility (CSR) considers many ethical quandaries when it comes to doing the right thing. Often these are not straightforward, and are subject to change over time, as new knowledge impacts on the workplace.

Measurement

Having briefly touched on the above we now focus on the 'what' and here is the first challenge, what to measure? We offer caution on some of the adverse impacts that measurement may have on the workforce and suggest tools that can be used. Surveys such as ASSET can simplify this for you, along with other common workforce metrics such as sickness absence. Measurement needs careful consideration and there are many areas you can focus on. Having clarity about what you want to know is key. Also, creating an environment in which you can stop measurements that are causing more problems than they are resolving is also preferable, relating to many aspects we have discussed already in this book, such as culture and engagement.

Data

With new legislation, and old legislation trying to keep up with new working technologies, we provide an overview of data collection, though this is covered in further detail in our final chapter.

Effectiveness

This explores if your organization is doing what it claims to be doing, or, doing it well. Used in tandem with our next sub-heading this applies to what the business is setting out to do. For example, the main aim of the business may be to produce X; however, there are that many processes and it is that bureaucratic, it ends up doing more of Y. Consider how to measure effectiveness.

Efficiency

Closely linked to effectiveness, efficiency relates to how an organization uses its own resources to be effective. You often hear the phrase *efficiency savings* to describe this. The important thing to remember here is that the human resources (ie the people) are most likely the most important part of this in the majority of companies. What you consider to be efficient needs to be established early on and reviewed if necessary. Most organizations change frequently, so adaptation is the key to keeping this relevant; your workforce will surely appreciate this.

Productivity

This area, along with our next, performance, may be where the investment in an effective wellbeing strategy is most felt, when the organization is working like a finely tuned instrument. This is usually because the workforce is fully engaged, drawing meaning and purpose from what they do, and as a direct result they, and the business, are productive. It is rare, we suggest, that you will find high employee wellbeing but poor productivity.

Performance

This can be a further lens to view the fruits of a good wellbeing strategy, with performance being optimal. Remember, you do not want to overstretch the workforce, so leave room in the plans for developmental opportunities, for innovation and for trying new ways of working. This ensures employee buy-in and is far more likely to result in high-performing organizations, teams and individuals.

Happiness

The happiness, or subjective wellbeing, of the workforce is paramount. The brain releases many chemicals that impact on the way a person feels, almost on a moment by moment basis. Although this is not a book on neuropsychology, it is important to recognize that meaning and purpose in working life bring about happiness. If the workforce experiences a deep sense of satisfaction in what they do (their state), you are more likely to have high levels of productivity and performance.

Evaluation

This area is concerned with critically reviewing what you have done, either internally or by a third party independently. As we have said, gold standard would be independent, but if done correctly an internal evaluation can be acceptable. The crux is to see if you have got things right – are you spending the right amount, investing the right amount of time, hiring the right people, promoting the right people? Evaluation needs to be carried out regularly, especially if you are trialling new ways of working, innovations, interventions and so on. Do not be afraid to change tack if the evaluation tells you that you are going off course – that is the whole point of it. We note that many funding opportunities caveat evaluation as a mandatory element, so it is worth thinking about at the start of any programme of work.

References

Ackoff, R (1999) *Ackoff's Best New York*, John Wiley & Sons, Chichester, pp 170–72

Balogun, J (2007) The practice of organizational restructuring: From design to reality, *European Management Journal*, **25** (2), pp 81–91

Collinson, D (2012) Prozac leadership and the limits of positive thinking, *Leadership*, **8** (2), pp 87–107

Craig, C L *et al* (2003) International physical activity questionnaire: 12-country reliability and validity, *Medicine and Science in Sports and Exercise*, **35** (8), pp 1381–95

Diener, E, Emmons, R A, Larsen, R J and Griffin, S (1985) The satisfaction with life scale, *Journal of Personality Assessment*, **49**, pp 71–75

Diener, E, Lucas, R and Oishi, S (2007) The optimum level of well-being, *Journal of Perspectives on Psychology Science*, **2** (4) pp 346–60

Eisenberger, R, Huntington, R, Hutchison, S and Sowa, D (1986) Perceived organizational support, *Journal of Applied Psychology*, **71**, pp 500–07

Faragher, E B, Cooper, C L and Cartwright, S (2004) A shortened stress evaluation tool (ASSET), *Stress and Health*, **20**, pp 189–201

Hesketh, I, Cooper, C and Ivy, J (2017) Well-being and engagement: The key to unlocking discretionary effort?, *Policing*, **11** (1), pp 62–73

Hesketh, I, Cooper, C and Ivy, J (2018) [accessed 4 August 2018] Leading the Asset: Resilience Training Efficacy in UK Policing, *Police Journal: Theory, Practice and Principles* [Online] http://journals.sagepub.com/toc/pjxa/0/0

Hills, P and Argyle, M (2002) The Oxford Happiness Questionnaire: A compact scale for the measurement of psychological well-being, *Personality and Individual Differences*, **33**, pp 1073–82

Johnson, G, Scholes, K and Whittington, R (2008) *Exploring Corporate Strategy*, 8th edn, Pearson Education, London

Lyubomirsky, S (2013) *The How of Happiness: A practical approach to getting the life you want*, Piatkus, London

Lyubomirsky, S and Lepper, H S (1999) A measure of subjective happiness: Preliminary reliability and construct validation, *Social Indicators Research*, **46**, pp 137–55

MacLeod, D and Clarke, N (2009) [accessed 4 August 2018] Engaging For Success: Enhancing Performance Through Employee Engagement, *Department for Business Innovation and Skills* [Online] http://www.engageforsuccess.org/wp-content/uploads/2012/09/file52215.pdf

Mayo, E (1946 [1933]) *The Human Problems of an Industrial Civilisation*, 2nd edn, Harvard University, Boston

Mintzberg, H (2009) Rebuilding companies as communities, *Harvard Business Review*, **87** (7, 8), pp 140–43

Mintzberg, H, Ahlstrand, B and Lampel, J (2008) *Strategy Safari: The complete guide through the wilds of strategic management*, Financial Times Prentice Hall, Harlow

Robertson Cooper Ltd (2017) What is a Good Day at Work? Wellbeing, expectations and experiences of work, Conference 28 March, Royal College of Physicians, London

Schwartz, S H (1996) Value priorities and behavior: Applying a theory of integrated value systems, in *The Psychology of Values: The Ontario Symposium*, vol 8, ed C Seligman, J M Olson and M P Zanna, pp 1–24, Erlbaum, Hillsdale, NJ

Smith, B W, Dalen, J, Wiggins, K, Tooley, E, Christopher, P and Bernard, J (2008) The Brief Resilience Scale: Assessing the ability to bounce back, *International Journal of Behavioral Medicine*, **15**, pp 194–200

Watson, D, Clark, L A and Tellegen, A (1988) Development and validation of brief measures of positive and negative affect: The PANAS scales, *Journal of Personality and Social Psychology*, **54**, pp 1063–70

Tools and legislation 06

Introduction

Returning to the purpose of this book, to help you design, implement and evaluate an effective wellbeing strategy for the workplace, this last chapter will hopefully equip you, or give you some ideas, on how to work through this process. We hope you may be able to use this part of the book as a reference for ideas, or as a manual to help colleagues understand better what it is you are trying to achieve, and also the benefits that this will bring to your people. As we have established, the extensive use of good wellbeing practices benefits your businesses performance and, of course, employee wellbeing. There is already extensive evidence from a variety of business sectors on the benefits that effective wellbeing brings for organizational performance, and emerging evidence from a variety of sectors on the benefits for employees. Good wellbeing practices enhance workers' skills, improve their motivation to perform well, and provide opportunities for workers to influence their work directly. These practices include having working environments that allow staff to have input into decisions about their work and their wider working environment. We will discuss team exercises that can tease these out of employees later in this chapter. Good wellbeing practices also support workers with access to learning and development opportunities, feedback on their work through good performance management systems and encourage managers to support those they manage.

Chapter 5, with a focus on monitoring and evaluation, will hopefully have provided you with information on the key terms, the approach and how to view and assess what you are proposing, or already doing. In this final chapter we provide a series of quick tools to help you identify and resolve both long- and short-term people challenges, as well as thinking about more adventurous people-related initiatives drawn from industry innovators. This toolkit will allow use of this book as a reference guide to call upon when issues arise in the workplace that you are not quite sure how to address, or resolve. It will also help you to establish health-supporting work conditions and clarify processes such as attendance policies, management exception criteria (eg for compassionate leave or special circumstances) and other pay-related matters.

We explore legislative requirements, what may be considered employer responsibilities and those that could be considered the responsibility of the employee. Of course, this will be dependent on where in the globe you are operating, but nonetheless legislation is introduced usually to protect people, either from an organization, danger, or themselves. European working-time directives are a good example of this. To be clear, we see all wellbeing as a contract between individuals and their respective organizations. There has to be give and take here, otherwise this is unlikely to be successful. For example, businesses can hardly be expected to provide facilities to improve the health and wellbeing of their charges if people do not use them or make lifestyle choices that put their general health at risk. This is true in reverse also, so it is very much along the lines of what we would describe as a psychological contract.

We also champion the notion that most wellbeing initiatives involve combinations of multiple approaches and stakeholders, and it is the joint working that really makes them work effectively; this is often what is compelling. With that in mind we have provided example exercises that can be done by employees, by groups or teams, and ones that can be carried out organization-wide. Using these you can look where your gaps may be, what causes concern for people, and what may leave your organization sub-optimal.

Tools

Strategy creation

Although we have discussed strategy in Chapter 3 and again briefly in Chapter 5, it is worth revisiting to look specifically at this in relation to the tools aspect. A good way to get rolling with your strategy is to *board-blast* with key people in your organization, and from that try to create a plan. Board-blasting, or brain-storming, is a way of getting quick-fire thoughts from people to capture what is foremost in their minds at a given point without them having to give too much thought. What is primary when a topic is introduced? An example is provided in Figure 6.1, where we detail some of the many elements you can consider when creating a wellbeing strategy.

We recommend that you start by looking at what is available to you, both internally and externally. Who is prepared to help? Can you ask local educational institutions to assist? These are resources that can provide both independent and up-to-date information that may assist you greatly. Many public-sector organizations now collaborate closely with their local and national educators, co-producing initiatives for the workforce, and public good. Another outlet is existing information, held on internal systems. However, you may be wise to first read our guidance later in this chapter. Also, the reason for unions or staff associations is predominantly to arrange the best working conditions for their members, so these too are willing participants in any wellbeing initiatives you may be considering. This may also be useful in bringing down barriers and facilitating closer working relationships.

The second part of Figure 6.1 illustrates some of the mechanisms for delivery that you may wish to consider, for example how are you going to communicate your approach, what will be the engagement strategy accompanying your plans? The final element of the process is the important area of evaluation and, of course, we see this as a continuous process. This example is by no means exhaustive and is intended to give you a little insight in where to go to garner information that you may find useful.

Like most things, you may find the starting point the most difficult. All the elements are detailed in this book, and you may find it useful to create your own diagrammatical representation to fit your own organization's specifics. We suggest you ground the basis of your approach in robust academic research. This is mainly so that you have a good foundation for all you do in terms of wellbeing. We also recommend you consult widely in the first instance, and then hone down

Figure 6.1   An example of a graphical representation of your wellbeing strategy

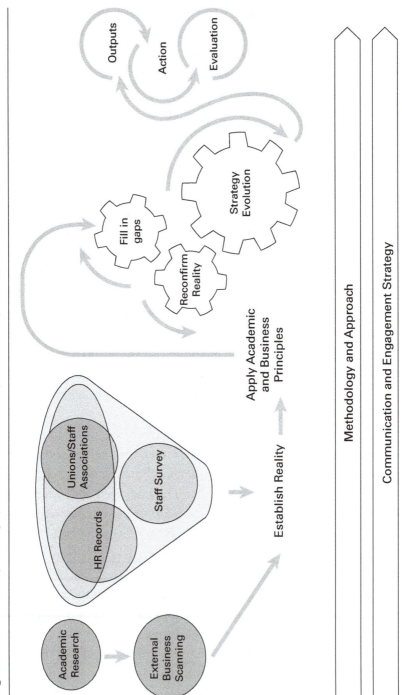

with key actors in your plans. Allow these to create a vision congruent with the organization, as we have discussed in previous chapters. Then, when you are happy, consult again.

It is critical you get the start right, and as many people on board as is possible. Our experience has been that in terms of business strategy, wellbeing is usually received with open arms. This is, in large part, because there are not many downsides to it. Most people welcome the notion that an organization is setting out to make their working environment as comfortable as possible, is concerned with their welfare, and is giving them an identity and a clear meaning and purpose. Further, that the organization values good leadership and the criticality of understanding personal resilience. There would need to be some serious downsides to dilute this vision for the workforce.

Wellbeing toolkits

Toolkits can be a really useful way of socializing your wellbeing strategy in the workplace and provide a clear guide, some advice and techniques, to help the workforce with wellbeing. They give all those involved in your organization a chance to see for themselves, to get involved and try things out. We have previously written them for other organizations (eg policing) and they have proven to be excellent internal reference documents. An important aspect is that you set off a conversation about wellbeing. Sometimes this will be met with suspicion, or even trepidation, but don't be alarmed, our experience tells us that things soon settle and people start to suggest good ways of working, or improvements in existing practice. Suggestions will hopefully concur with areas you are testing out or trialling, pilot projects and so on. The idea is that you craft these for whatever organizational context you operate in, and tailor the wellbeing approaches you are intending to take to suit your own industry's operating environment. That way, you can catch the nuances that may be particular to your own line of work.

In order to achieve success organizations rely heavily on their workforce feeling involved, valued and engaged. Of course, organizations also rely heavily on people to make sense of these resources, and that is where great leaders come into play – those with the energy, attitude and capability to interpret, empower and encourage, and to make real the initiatives proposed. One last point is that toolkits should not be too generic but should draw on good practice and specify how they fit a particular organizational context.

Organizational exercises

It is useful to carry out some sort of baseline assessment before you begin any interventions or programmes of work. It may also be useful to carry out periodic checkpoints to consider where you are, where you have come from, and if you are going in the right (intended) direction. We will consider here what these may each involve. This work is closely linked with evaluation and will undoubtedly feature in any subsequent evaluation work that is carried out. These considerations will assist you to determine what people are available to you in the workplace, and if they are skilled in what you require them to do. To explain this further, with the fast pace of change we often see this as critical to success, ie organizations have a willing and capable workforce, however the workforce is not skilled in the tasks the company is proposing to undertake. Does this sound familiar? One of the problematic outcomes of this is that it is stressful for all, workers and managers. So, you may first ask the question, what are the mission and goals of the organization with regards to future work? What support can the senior management and managers give towards this work? Are there development needs, or training requirements to enable the current workforce to do this work? Is the organization supportive and on-board with processes to adapt? Are there adequate resources currently available, or plans to develop these? All these considerations help you to shape the wellbeing strategy and make it proportionate to the future direction of the business.

Team exercises

At first glance you may be drawn to physical exercise, and that is not a bad start point. The idea of training classes highlights that people, as social beings, draw strength and enjoyment from team sports. This can also transfer into psychological wellbeing, where a sense of community makes us feel better within ourselves. To that extent, focus groups, team away days and collaborative learning sets are popular for a very good reason. We mentioned the Hawthorne studies earlier in the book, and this was one of the key findings in those studies. That is, the workforce establishes the general feeling of belonging and comradery in the organization. Carefully facilitated this can provide valuable input in whatever you embark upon. What is more, it enables you to look at capability in terms of your workforce, and to make an initial assessment of what may become barriers to success, or even blockers. Having regular meets where people are discussed, and not in a critical way but in a supportive and developmental orientation, is vital. Carefully facilitated, you can draw out quality feedback on working initiatives and other plans incorporated in your overall wellbeing strategy.

Individual exercises

To ascertain how much individuals value their own career and current life choices, you can do exercises to help clarify. This example of such an exercise has a focus on purpose. An approach to thinking about your life purpose is to write a newspaper article that you hope to read about yourself in five years' time. What would the headline say? What would be the strap line underneath? What would the article say about you, your achievements and your purpose? When you write your article don't just think about work-related news, think about your whole life. This is a fairly quick exercise that puts you in a bubble, thinking solely about your own role and purpose in life. Reflective practices like this can help clarify what is important to individuals, and it may well be that they value their family contribution foremost, and the salary, location and job itself facilitates their home life. In other words, don't forget this may be at a point in time where family commitments take precedence. Also, this may well change, so it is good practice to repeat this over time.

There are many online documents and exercises that effectively look at the same sort of approach. Take, for example, training needs analysis (TNAs), or development needs analysis (DNAs) tools. It should be noted that these can be employees, organizational and a team assessment tool also, so are highly desirable as part of any initial assessment, or baselining, you may be considering. You can also combine these with cost benefit analysis tools and exercises to seek out where your gaps are, and how best to fill them. Can these gaps be filled by training existing employees, for example, or are they best done through new hires? These are all exercises you can do with individuals or teams to tease out how best to integrate your people capabilities into your wellbeing strategy. Of course, such information could also be useful to bear in mind when creating a personalized wellbeing plan.

Good practice

Workplace stressors

The UK Health and Safety Executive (HSE) reported that 12.5 million working days were lost to absence caused by stress, anxiety and depression in 2016/17 in the UK, and that stress, anxiety and depression accounted for 49 per cent of all working days lost due to ill health in the UK (HSE, 2017). The HSE website is a great resource to reference factors that impact on people's working life in respect of a whole range of issues. These include shift work and fatigue, health surveillance, work-related stress, drugs and alcohol, and violence at work. The list of issues could fill a whole book on its own, but what we are interested in here are the management standards that address six key workplace themes that are known to impact on wellbeing in most occupations, as illustrated in Figure 6.2. These standards, as

Figure 6.2   The Health and Safety Executive (UK) six management standards

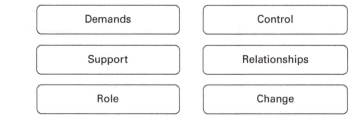

Demands	Control
Support	Relationships
Role	Change

SOURCE HSE (2018)

you will see, are generic and portable to most industry sectors. They also form the basis of many wellbeing question sets, with slight subtleties being added here and there. In terms of a point of reference, or a tool, they are useful.

1 The first of these areas of work design is in addressing demands. These include shift work and the working environment. The actual standard that the HSE recommends includes the ability of an employee to be able to cope with the demands that are placed upon them in the role they are performing. This is congruent with our earlier observations on creating the right working environment, and you can also see how the element of personal resilience plays a huge part here. The thrust of this is that you also ensure there are mechanisms in place to allow employees to challenge their demands reasonably. That is, to prevent them being overworked, which leads to burnout, absenteeism, presenteeism and leaveism.

2 Closely linked is the second element, that of control. Again, the focus is on the employee and how much say they have in their work. As in our ASSET questions, discussed earlier in this book, control is a key ingredient in terms of worker identity, and gives employees a sense of ownership in their work. With this comes pride and energy, as they feel they are making a meaningful contribution to the direction of the business. Contrary to this, when there is little or no control on offer, an employee may feel lethargic and disengage.

3 Support is the next area that can be a source of stress in the workplace, feeling unsupported or even isolated. This may be particularly pertinent to remote or lone workers, those working flexibly, from home or out on the road. The questions here are centred around organizational support, and where that comes from. For example, are people matrix-managed or do they have consistent line management that is supportive and developmental? The age of technology has 'algorithmed out' some of the line management, making a case for efficiency and streamlining. The result, on some occasions, has been that layers of management may have been removed. This can leave people feeling vulnerable or uncared for. Support is an important aspect for people to feel

secure and worthwhile, and again, meaning and purpose come strongly into play. So, the questions are, do you know who your line manager is? (We hope we cross this bridge.) Followed by, how much contact do you have with them? This can be the stumbling block, so regular planned meetings or contact are advised. It is also good practice to let employees know what sort of contact they may expect, what their expectations may be, and what will work for both parties. Although this may seem relatively trivial, survey after survey reports poor line-manager support. As the line manager has probably the biggest impact on your wellbeing at work, it is important to get this right.

4 Our work relationships are the next key issue, and as you will start to grasp, these elements are all closely related. Feeling part of the whole is important to employees, and relationships with colleagues are important. Dependent on home circumstances, these can be the major social contact that people have. Because the majority of readers will most likely spend a good percentage of their waking hours at work, you can see how bonds form within the working environment. Inevitably, with any close bonds there may become points of friction, and here the recommendations are that strict policies regarding acceptable behaviour, ethical conduct, bullying (often dismissed as banter) and so on, are effectively managed. These may include resolution processes or sanctions for behaviour. Equally, you may reward behaviours that champion your vision and plans for the company, which are often more effective in any case.

5 A person's role within the business is the next area to consider, including how this is established. Theories of organizational fairness come into play here (Greenberg, 1987). These include how roles are established, how people are recruited or promoted into them, and what the exit plans are if roles are disestablished. All these issues can play on the minds of employees, potentially disrupting the workplace. Emotional exhaustion, health issues, turnover intention, absence and withdrawal, counter-productive work behaviours and job satisfaction have all been linked to fairness in the workplace, so it is one to ignore at your peril.

Once again, we recommend that your wellbeing strategy includes plans in this respect, or that it reviews existing policies to account for new knowledge in this area of business.

6 The final element under this good-practice section is that of managing change, and although we have touched on this already within this book, it is nevertheless an important aspect of work. Almost all workforces go through programmes of change, and nearly all that do report poor management practices on that journey. Delivering change programmes is well established in today's workplace, so this should not be as difficult as first it may appear. As with all things, there needs to be a focus on people, and the affect that change has on them, both individually and as teams, departments or functions. One of the key aspects to any change programme is effective communication. Letting those who will be impacted upon, in any way, know that an organization is restructuring or reviewing an area of business is much more likely to result in improved working relationships moving forward. We suggest this even if there are job reductions on the cards. We extend this to contractors and suppliers also. People are often the best asset an organization has and using their collective experience and knowledge can result in smooth change programmes, so is a worthwhile consideration. One of the most stressful aspects of working in an organization is experienced when change programmes are implemented.

Change seldom happens all of a sudden, with no prior warning. Employees often see that something needs to change, either to cope with the latest innovation, or to keep up with competitors. As an organization tries to achieve its goals, it is incumbent on the workforce to work together and with other people, inside the organization and out. Having the wherewithal to change productively, you are much more likely to get the help that allows you to change and grow successfully. If you try to change without bringing your workforce along with you, you may find it extremely difficult or you may even fail. Direction and goals can quickly slip out of reach. Effective change can mean the difference between being championed and being incapacitated.

Legislation

Rules on data collection

One of the most important ways to check up on your wellbeing strategy is to ask the workforce. However, this also comes with some important implications and considerations for the organization. Because it is vital that you do this we will now look at the parameters within which you can do it. Here we will outline some of the recommendations, based on the guidance from the Information Commissioner's Office (UK), born out of the General Data Protection Regulation (GDPR), which although is a European directive, we suggest is equally relevant wherever you are in the world (EUGDPR, 2018). Compliance with the GDPR really amounts to ethical practice that should feature in any corporate social responsibility plan.

The first point to consider, as with most communications issues within organizations, is that of awareness. Organizations should make sure that those charged with the collection and use of personal data are aware of the legislation. This really is just good practice, but is commonly overlooked, only surfacing when things go wrong, or are challenged. There needs to be an appreciation of the impact that the data collection will have, perhaps via risk assessment. Most medium- or large-sized organizations carry risk registers as good practice. Also, do not underestimate the amount of work this may introduce into your organization. Compliance is a growing industry!

When you collect information from people, which is inevitable as you ascertain what is effective within your wellbeing strategy, you need to inform those who you collect it from. This should also go some way to explaining who is collecting, what form, what sharing protocols are in place and your intended use.

The following point to consider is what data (information) you are storing, where it came from, and who you are sharing it with (if anyone). Best practice would suggest you establish this across the organization and document what you have done, who you have told and your future compliance processes. If in the EU, the GDPR requires you to maintain records of your processing activities, and to be able to account how you have complied with the requirements.

You should also check your procedures to ensure they cover all the rights that individuals have, including how you would delete personal data or provide data electronically and in a commonly used format. The rights of individuals are central to the GDPR and includes their right to be informed, have access, and to have information rectified or erased. What is interesting is that this also includes the right not to be subjected to automated decision making, which includes profiling. This may well impact on automated processes that effectively do this to filter people, such as those involved in HR screening and so on.

What will immediately be apparent here is the need to work out how all this will fit in as you set your strategy going, and how you effectively plan to deal with requests of this nature. This legislation more or less prohibits charging for information requests, so there may be an added expense if people request information on a regular basis. Of course, one way you can deal with this is to make information available online. You cannot assume consent either, you must have this expressly given.

One of the key points of this issue is that a lot of organizations will not have a lawful basis for processing personal data. However, this will be different under the GDPR because some individuals' rights will be modified depending on your lawful basis for processing their personal data. The most obvious example is that people will have a stronger right to have their data deleted where you use consent as your lawful basis for processing, ie you are not doing anything with it other than holding it because they consented to that. You will also have to explain your lawful basis for processing personal data in a 'privacy notice' and when you answer a subject access request. The lawful bases in the GDPR are broadly the same as the conditions for processing in the Data Protection Act (DPA). It should be possible to review the types of processing activities you carry out and to identify your lawful basis for doing so.

If your organization has anything to do with children, the way you deal with their data has further restrictions. You should be thinking about whether you need to put systems in place to verify individuals' ages and to obtain parental or guardian consent for any data-processing activity. The GDPR brings special protection for children's personal data, particularly in the context of commercial internet services such as social networking. If your organization offers online services to children and relies on consent to collect information about them, then you may need a parent or guardian's consent in order to process their personal data lawfully. The GDPR sets the age when a child can give their own consent to this processing at 16 (although this may be lowered to a minimum of 13 in the UK). If a child is younger then you will need to get consent from a person holding 'parental responsibility'. You should remember that consent has to be verifiable and that when collecting children's data your privacy notice must be written in language that children will understand.

If you have breaches in personal data you need to report these. It therefore follows that you should have the correct procedures in place to do this. It is good practice to designate a person to deal with data protection, and formally recognize this role within your wellbeing strategy. This also indicates to your workforce that you really value their privacy and respect their wishes in terms of what they disclose. You will see that this can be conflicting, in one respect you wish people to be open and honest, and on the other hand you are throwing a veil over disclosure, ie hiding it from clear view. It is a complex world in which we live.

Health and safety

We increasingly see organizations aligning wellbeing to health and safety. Although they may seem to be a perfect fit, we urge caution on one or two fronts. If we take a look at health and safety legislation, for example, you will quickly see that this more or less amounts to a list of prohibition. What you should not do, what is illegal, what is advised against, and so on. The issue here is that these are largely negative, and mostly punitive. In terms of wellbeing, your optimum approach will come from positivity – talking, behaving, promoting and exampling models that bring about meaning and purpose in the workplace. Although health and safety has brought about beneficial change for organizations, we do not see wellbeing fitting perfectly, as an extension of health and safety. Organizational development, if your company has such a function, is probably the best place. People directorates, HR or L&D are other faculties where wellbeing can sit comfortably. Occupational health, again dependent on the size of your organization, is another favourite for wellbeing to sit, but again we urge caution. Here, we are not suggesting wellbeing deals with people who are unwell. What we actually wish to achieve is proactivity in the workplace. Occupational health, in many respects, is a reactive function. If your occupational health function is entirely proactive, however, this may be the perfect place. Most, unfortunately, are not. All of these functions will be interested in wellbeing, and all have their part to play in the strategy. You will find that policies and procedures, legislation and local customs (ways of working) will all impact on wellbeing, which is why we devoted a significant amount of this book to discussing culture.

In terms of legislation, most countries have health and safety regulations that protect their workforces from bad or dangerous practice, and these can include sub-topics such as labour laws or working-time directives, as previously mentioned. By way of example, the HSE has fined organizations for numerous breaches of health and safety legislation in the UK, and regularly publishes these sanctions online. We are not going to list them, but needless to say the majority are in place to protect the workforce. It should also be noted that most employee law is brought about as a result of something going wrong previously. That is, they are post-incident responses to ensure things do not happen again to the detriment of the workforce. In the majority of medium-plus-sized companies, staff associations or unions will support health and safety functions, ensuring business owners are compliant. These protections for the workforce are generally positive in terms of wellbeing, as they allow us to focus on the people attributes that make a big difference in attitudes and perceptions in the workplace.

It is important to distinguish between health and safety, occupational health and wellbeing. Although they may be under the same management, we suggest they are quite unique, especially in what we are trying to achieve. The design, implementation and evaluation of your wellbeing strategy may include all of these elements in one form or another. However, we caution against merging as they require a very different approach in terms of how they are viewed by the workforce. We suggest wellbeing is always positively framed, is a living and dynamic part of your business and continually improving – wellbeing is seen by all as a necessary and worthwhile part of their employment. We hope you can see the differences in this respect.

Summary

The overall purpose of this book has been to help you design, implement and evaluate an effective wellbeing strategy for your workplace. This chapter has hopefully provided you with the last pieces of the jigsaw to do that. One of the key aims of this chapter, and the book overall, has been to give you a set of references, or tools, to refer to when developing and implementing your wellbeing strategy. The integrated use of good wellbeing practices will undoubtedly benefit your business's performance, productivity and, of course, employee wellbeing. We have made the point several times during this book that there is already extensive evidence from a variety of business sectors on the benefits that effective wellbeing brings for organizational performance and, together with emerging evidence from a variety of sectors on the benefits for employees, this makes for a compelling motivation to adopt the practices we have outlined in this book.

Good wellbeing practices enhance workers' skills, improve their motivation to perform well, and provide opportunities for workers to influence their work directly. To recap, these practices include having working environments that allow staff to have input into decisions about their work and their wider working environment. In this final chapter we have also touched on exercises that can tease these out of employees, whether that be individually, in teams, or as an organization. It should be noted that good wellbeing practices also support workers with access to L&D opportunities, feedback on their work through good performance management systems and encourage managers to actively support those they manage.

Also included in this final chapter are a series of quick tools to help you identify and resolve both long- and short-term people challenges, as well as thinking about more adventurous people-related initiatives drawn from industry innovators. These suggestions will allow the use of this book as a reference guide to call upon when issues arise in the workplace that you are not quite sure how to address, or resolve. It will also help you to establish health-supporting work conditions and clarify processes such as attendance policies, exceptions and pay-related matters.

We have also taken a look at some major legislative requirements that cannot be ignored as you embark on a wellbeing strategy, or wish to review an existing wellbeing strategy. These cover what may be considered employer responsibilities and those that could be considered the responsibility of the employee. Of course, this will be dependent on where in the globe you are operating, but nonetheless legislation is introduced usually to protect people, either from an organization, danger, or themselves. European working-time directives are a good example of this. To reiterate our point here, we see all wellbeing as a contract between individuals and their respective organizations. There has to be give and take, otherwise your wellbeing strategy is unlikely to be successful.

We conclude with the notion that most wellbeing plans sit with other sub-departments or faculties, some of which may not provide best fit. We offer some rationale and advice to help you decide where best to site your wellbeing strategy within the domains of your business. Wellbeing often involves combinations of multiple approaches and stakeholders, and it is the joint working and network that really makes it work effectively. Therefore, we argue that to get the very best out of your wellbeing strategy it is vital to consider internal ownership and accountability.

Final key takeaways and considerations

Strategy creation

Consider what evidence you already have, what information you may need, what to do with it, and of course how to evaluate. We suggest you set off with evaluation in mind and provide a few tips about the considerations you need to process.

Wellbeing toolkits

These are an excellent way to land the strategy in the workplace and provide a clear guide, some advice and techniques to help the workforce with wellbeing. We have previously written them for other organizations and they have proven to be excellent internal reference documents. The idea is that you craft these for whatever organizational context you operate in, and tailor the wellbeing approaches you are intending to take to suit your own industry's operating environment. That way you can catch the nuances that may be particular to your own line of work. Toolkits should not be too generic but should draw on good practice and specify how they fit a particular organizational context.

Organizational exercises

These can help you prepare and identify gaps in current provision. They also allow you to take an overview of your organizational needs, in terms of resources, development opportunities and future plans and contingencies. Often based on needs-analysis exercises, there are numerous frameworks you can use to map out your current position. We suggest this is done with executive stakeholders in the first instance, and then cascaded down, socializing your ideas with the broader workforce and requesting feedback. Often termed Delphi rounds, this technique will help you establish a strategy that the workforce will buy into and take ownership of along the way.

Team exercises

Teams of individuals can form groups, similar to learning sets, that can work through issues and challenges via professional discussion. Carefully facilitated, you can draw out quality feedback on working initiatives and other plans incorporated in your overall wellbeing strategy. These are, of course, considerations and there is no mandate to do everything. This will very much depend on the size of your workforce, and the locations of your employees, who may be spread over a wide geographical area.

Individual exercises

When we look at meaning and purpose in life, it means so many things to different people. We would argue that no two people have the same goals, though they may be similar enough to line up for a cause, or a movement. Trying to establish what drives individuals in your organization can provide you with key insight into how you might implement your wellbeing strategy. Finding the common ground, but valuing difference, is what this exercise is about. What are the issues on which the majority agree? Where are you going to achieve buy-in? All are excellent questions to ask and consider within your strategy.

Good practice

We promote the practice of looking at what has worked in other sectors of industry. There are many online tools you can use from around the world that can help you compare and contrast with your own organizational needs. We provide an example from the UK Health and Safety Executive here, but there are many others you can draw on, such as the US Department of Labor website (DoL, 2018) or the Australian Institute of Health and Welfare website (AIHW, 2018).

Legislation

It is important within the operating environment to recognize the legal frameworks in which you do business. Depending on relative size, and the country in which you operate, you will undoubtedly have legal parameters to work within in terms of the treatment of employees, contractors and so on. We pick up on the thorny issue of data collection, storage and use in this section, and also touch a little on health and safety legislation. Working-time directives are another area you need to consider, as well as travel issues such as driving and rest periods for workers, annual leave, sickness pay, maternity and so on. It is wise to consider how legal requirements fit into your wellbeing strategy. A positive move is to feature these as benefits and recognition of the support and work ethic of your employees. This will bring about good engagement and is likely to return higher levels of productivity and performance, as with all good wellbeing approaches.

References

AIHW (2018) [accessed 17 April 2018] Australian Institute of Health and Welfare [Online] https://www.aihw.gov.au

DoL (2018) [accessed 17 April 2018] United States Department of Labor [Online] https://www.dol.gov

EUGDPR (2018) [accessed 17 April 2018] EU General Data Protection Regulation [Online] https://www.eugdpr.org

Greenberg, J (1987) A taxonomy of organizational justice theories, *Academy of Management Review*, **12**, pp 9–22

HSE (2017) [accessed 17 April 2018] Work-related Stress, Depression or Anxiety Statistics in Great Britain 2017 [Online] http://www.hse.gov.uk/statistics/causdis/stress/stress.pdf

HSE (2018) [accessed 17 April 2018] Management Standards [Online] http://www.hse.gov.uk/stress/standards/role.htm

REFERENCES

Ackoff, R (1999) *Ackoff's Best New York*, John Wiley & Sons, Chichester, pp 170–72

Age in the Workplace (2016) [accessed 4 August 2018] [Online] http://age.bitc.org.uk

AIHW (2018) [accessed 17 April 2018] Australian Institute of Health and Welfare [Online] https://www.aihw.gov.au

Balogun, J (2007) The practice of organizational restructuring: From design to reality, *European Management Journal*, **25** (2), pp 81–91

Balogun, J and Hope-Hailey, V (2008) *Exploring Strategic Change*, 3rd edn, Prentice Hall, Harlow

Bass, B (1985) *Leadership and Performance Beyond Expectations*, Free Press, New York

Bennis, W G (1989) *On Becoming a Leader*, Century, London

BITC (2016a) [accessed 4 August 2018] Royal Mail Group – Feeling First Class [Online] https://www.bitc.org.uk/resources-training/case-studies/royal-mail-group-feeling-first-class

BITC (2016b) [accessed 4 August 2018] Leading on Mental Wellbeing – Transforming the Role of Line Managers: A Blueprint for Unlocking Employee Mental Wellbeing and Productivity [Online] https://wellbeing.bitc.org.uk/system/files/research/bitc_linemanagerreport_feb2016_final.pdf

Burns, J (1978) *Leadership*, Harper & Rowe, New York

Calnan, M (2017) [accessed 4 August 2018] One in Four Employees With Mental Health Issues Say Work is the Cause, *People Management*, 28 March [Online] http://www2.cipd.co.uk/pm/peoplemanagement/b/weblog/ archive/2017/03/28/one-in-four-employees-with-mental-healthissues- say-work-is-the-cause.aspx

Carpenter, L (2017) [accessed 4 August 2018] The CEO of Lloyds Bank Turned its Fortunes Around – But the Anxiety Almost Broke Him, *The Times*, 7 October [Online] https://www.thetimes.co.uk/article/the-ceoof-lloyds-bank-turned-its-fortunes-around-but-the-anxiety-almostbroke-him-fg970cpjr

Casey, G W (2014) Leading in a VUCA world, *Fortune*, **169** (5), p 75

CIPD (2017) [accessed 31 July 2018] One million more older people need to be in work by 2022 [Online] https://www.cipd.co.uk/news-views/news-articles/million-more-older-workers-needed

Collingridge, J, Shipman, T and Pogrund, G (2017) [accessed 4 August 2018] Labour Hushes Up Second 'Suicide' After Sex Claims, *The Times* [Online] https://www.thetimes.co.uk/article/labour-hushes-up-secondsuicide- after-sex-claims-zz950mwgt

Collinson, D (2012) Prozac leadership and the limits of positive thinking, *Leadership*, **8** (2), pp 87–107

Cowley, Science (2016) [accessed 31 July 2018] Future of Ageing: Seminar on Older Workers [Online] https://www.gov.uk/government/publications/future-of-ageing-seminar-on-older-workers

Craig, C L *et al* (2003) International physical activity questionnaire: 12-country reliability and validity, *Medicine and Science in Sports and Exercise*, **35** (8), pp 1381–95

Csikszentmihalyi, M (1992) *Flow: The psychology of happiness*, Rider, London

Diener, E, Emmons, R A, Larsen, R J and Griffin, S (1985) The satisfaction with life scale, *Journal of Personality Assessment*, **49**, pp 71–75

Diener, E, Lucas, R and Oishi, S (2007) The optimum level of well-being, *Journal of Perspectives on Psychology Science*, **2** (4) pp 346–60

DoL (2018) [accessed 17 April 2018] United States Department of Labor [Online] https://www.dol.gov

Downton, J (1973) *Rebel Leadership: Commitment and charisma in a revolutionary process*, Free Press, New York

Dweck, C S (2006) *Mindset: The new psychology of success*, 1st edn, Random House, New York

Eisenberger, R, Huntington, R, Hutchison, S and Sowa, D (1986) Perceived organizational support, *Journal of Applied Psychology*, **71**, pp 500–07

EUGDPR (2018) [accessed 17 April 2018] EU General Data Protection Regulation [Online] https://www.eugdpr.org

Faragher, E B, Cooper, C L and Cartwright, S (2004) A shortened stress evaluation tool (ASSET), *Stress and Health*, **20**, pp 189–201

Francke, A (2017) Walk and talk: your management must-dos, *Professional Manager*, Chartered Management Institute

Greenberg, J (1987) A taxonomy of organizational justice theories, *Academy of Management Review*, **12**, pp 9–22

Guilfoyle, S (2013) *Intelligent Policing: How systems thinking methods eclipse conventional management practice*, Triarchy Press, Devon

Haglund, M E M, Nestadt, P S, Cooper, N S, Southwick, S M and Charney, D S (2007) Psychobiological mechanisms of resilience: Relevance to prevention and treatment of stress-related psychopathology, *Dev Psychopathol*, **19** (3), pp 889–920

Hardy, B, Graham, R, Stansall, P, White, A, Harrison, A, Bell, A and Hutton, L (2008) *Working Beyond Walls: The government workplace as an agent of change*, DEGW/Office of Government Commerce, London [Online] https://assets.publishing.service.gov.uk/government/uploads/system/uploads/attachment_data/file/394153/Working-beyond-Walls.pdf

Hesketh, I, Cooper, C and Ivy, J (2017) Well-being and engagement: The key to unlocking discretionary effort?, *Policing*, **11** (1), pp 62–73

Hesketh, I, Cooper, C and Ivy, J (2018) [accessed 4 August 2018] Leading the Asset: Resilience Training Efficacy in UK Policing, *Police Journal: Theory, Practice and Principles* [Online] http://journals.sagepub.com/toc/pjxa/0/0

Hills, P and Argyle, M (2002) The Oxford Happiness Questionnaire: A compact scale for the measurement of psychological well-being, *Personality and Individual Differences*, **33**, pp 1073–82

Hood, C (1991) A public management for all seasons?, *Public Administration*, **69** (1), pp 3–19

HSE (2017) [accessed 17 April 2018] Work-related Stress, Depression or Anxiety Statistics in Great Britain 2017 [Online] http://www.hse.gov.uk/statistics/causdis/stress/stress.pdf

HSE (2018) [accessed 17 April 2018] Management Standards [Online] http://www.hse.gov.uk/stress/standards/role.htm

Johnson, G, Scholes, K and Whittington, R (2008) *Exploring Corporate Strategy*, 8th edn, Pearson Education, London

Johnston, R and Clark, G (2008) *Service Operations Management*, 3rd edn, Pearson Education, London

Judge, T A and Bono, J E (2000) Five-factor model of personality and transformational leadership, *Journal of Applied Psychology*, **85** (5), pp 751–65

Kandel, E (2017) [accessed 4 August 2018] Identical Twins – Not Identical Brains: Cold Spring Harbor Laboratory [Online] https://www.dnalc.org/view/1200-Identical-Twins-Not-Identical-Brains.html

Kuhn, T S (2012) *The Structure of Scientific Revolutions*, 4th edn, University of Chicago Press, Chicago and London Schein, E H (2010) *Organizational Culture and Leadership*, 4th edn, Jossey-Bass, San Francisco

Lau, J Y F (2011) *An Introduction to Critical Thinking and Creativity: Think More, Think Better*, Wiley, Hoboken, NJ

Luthans, F (2002) The need for and meaning of positive organizational behavior, *Journal of Organizational Behaviour*, **23** (6), pp 695–706

Lyubomirsky, S (2010) *The How of Happiness: A practical approach to getting the life you want*, Piatkus, London

Lyubomirsky, S (2013) *The How of Happiness: A practical approach to getting the life you want*, Piatkus, London

Lyubomirsky, S and Lepper, H S (1999) A measure of subjective happiness: Preliminary reliability and construct validation, *Social Indicators Research*, **46**, pp 137–55

MacLeod, D and Clarke, N (2009) [accessed 4 August 2018] Engaging For Success: Enhancing Performance Through Employee Engagement, *Department for Business Innovation and Skills* [Online] http://www.engageforsuccess.org/wp-content/uploads/2012/09/file52215.pdf

Mallack, L (1998) Measuring resilience in health care provider organizations, *Health Manpower Management*, **24** (4), pp 148–52

Masten, A S (2014) Global perspectives on resilience in children and youth, *Child Development*, **85** (1), pp 6–20

Mayo, E (1946 [1933]) *The Human Problems of an Industrial Civilisation*, 2nd edn, Harvard University, Boston

Medland, D (2017) [accessed 31 July 2017] Engage your core: The secret of Grant Thornton's new-found strength, *CMI* [Online] https://www. managers.org.uk/insights/news/2017/may/the-secret-to-grant-thorntonsnewfound-strength

Milligan-Saville, J *et al* (2017) Workplace mental health training for managers and its effect on sick leave in employees: A cluster randomised controlled trial, *Lancet Psychiatry*, **4**, pp 850–58

Mintzberg, H (2008) *Strategy Safari: The complete guide through the wilds of strategic management*, Financial Times Prentice Hall, Harlow

Mintzberg, H (2009) Rebuilding companies as communities, *Harvard Business Review*, **87** (7, 8), pp 140–43

Mintzberg, H, Ahlstrand, B and Lampel, J (2008) *Strategy Safari: The complete guide through the wilds of strategic management*, Financial Times Prentice Hall, Harlow

NICE (2017) [accessed 4 August 2018] Healthy Workplace: Improving Employee Mental and Physical Health and Wellbeing [Online] https://www.nice.org.uk/guidance/qs147

OECD (2012) [accessed 26 December 2012] Organization for Economic Cooperation and Development – Better Life Index [Online] www.oecdbetterlifeindex.org

Peters, S (2012) *The Chimp Paradox*, Vermilion, London

Porter, M and Kramer, R (2002) The competitive advantage of corporate philanthropy, *Harvard Business Review*, December

Rathus, S A (2012) *Psychology: Concepts and connections*, 10th edn, Wadsworth, Belmont, CA

Rhodes, A (2017) Speech at the Excellence in Policing Conference, Ryton, UK

Robertson, I, Cooper, C, Sarkar, M and Curran, T (2015) Resilience training in the workplace from 2003 to 2014: a systematic review, *Journal of Occupational Psychology*, **88** (3), pp 533–62

Robertson Cooper Ltd (2017) What is a Good Day at Work? Wellbeing, expectations and experiences of work, Conference 28 March, Royal College of Physicians, London

Schwartz, S H (1996) Value priorities and behavior: Applying a theory of integrated value systems, in *The Psychology of Values: The Ontario Symposium*, vol 8, ed C Seligman, J M Olson and M P Zanna, pp 1–24, Erlbaum, Hillsdale, NJ

Seligman, M (2003) *Authentic Happiness: Using the new positive psychology to realize your potential for deep fulfillment*, Nicholas Brealey, London

Seligman, M (2011) *Flourish: A new understanding of happiness and well-being – and how to achieve them*, Nicholas Brealey, London

Selye (1975) Confusion and controversy in the stress field, *Journal of Human Stress*, **1** (2), pp 37–44

Sinek, S (2009) *Start with Why*, Penguin, London

Smith, B W, Dalen, J, Wiggins, K, Tooley, E, Christopher, P and Bernard, J (2008) The Brief Resilience Scale: Assessing the ability to bounce back, *International Journal of Behavioral Medicine*, **15**, pp 194–200

Soane, E, Shantz, A, Alfes, K, Truss, C, Rees, C and Gatenby, M (2013) The association of meaningfulness, wellbeing, and engagement with absenteeism: A moderated mediation model, *Human Resource Management*, **52** (3), pp 441–56

Southwick, S and Charney, D (2012) *Resilience: The science of mastering life's greatest challenges*, Cambridge University Press, New York

Sullenberger, C (2012) *Making a Difference: Stories of vision and courage from America's leaders*, Harper Collins Publishers, New York

Syed, M (2015) *Black Box Thinking: Why most people never learn from their mistakes – but some do*, John Murray, London

Taft, M W (2017) [accessed 4 August 2018] Five live-enhancing insights from neuroscience [Online] https://www.brainreframe.org/singlepost/2016/02/04/Five-Life-Enhancing-Insights-from-Neuroscience

Thomson, P (2017) [accessed 31 July 2018] Fulfilling work is essential to supporting older workers, *Personnel Today* [Online] https://www.personneltoday.com/hr/fulfilling-work-essential-supportingolder-workers/

Vaillant, G (2003) *Aging Well: Surprising Guideposts to a happier life*, Little, Brown and Company, New York

Vernon, M (2017) Ageing well: Reducing unwarranted variation in health outcomes, lecture at the Open University, 25 September

Watson, D, Clark, L A and Tellegen, A (1988) Development and validation of brief measures of positive and negative affect: The PANAS scales, *Journal of Personality and Social Psychology*, **54**, pp 1063–70

de Wit, B (1994) *Strategy: Process, content and context an international perspective*, West, Saint Paul, MN

Wright, O (2017) [accessed 4 August 2018] Theresa May calls for new 'culture of respect' amid Westminster sleaze scandal, *The Times* [Online] https://www.thetimes.co.uk/article/theresa-may-calls-for-newculture-of-respect-amid-westminster-sleaze-scandal-6qv6x5fm9

INDEX

Note: page numbers in *italic* indicate figures or tables